DANIEL KOLAK, SERIES EDITOR

John Stuart Mill

On Liberty

EDITED BY MICHAEL B. MATHIAS

D0974640

PEARSON

Longman

New York • Boston • San Francisco
London • Toronto • Sydney • Tokyo • Singapore • Madrid
Mexico City • Munich • Paris • Cape Town • Hong Kong • Montreal

Editor in Chief:	Eric Stano
Senior Marketing Manager:	Ann Stypuloski
Production Coordinator:	Scarlett Lindsay
Text Design and Electronic Page Makeup:	Sunflower Publishing Services
Cover Designer/Manager:	John Callahan
Cover Illustration/Photo:	Courtesy of Getty Images, Inc.
Manufacturing Manager:	Mary Fischer
Manufacturing Buyer:	Roy Pickering
Printer and Binder:	R.R. Donnelley, Harrisonburg
Cover Printer:	Phoenix Color

Library of Congress Cataloging-in-Publication Data

John Stuart Mill : On liberty / edited by Michael B. Mathias.
    p. cm. -- (Longman library of primary sources in philosophy)
Includes bibliographical references.
ISBN 0-321-27614-0
1. Mill, John Stuart, 1806-1873. On liberty. 2. Liberty. I. Mathias, Michael B.
JC585.J64 2008
323.44--dc22

                                                      2006102686

Please visit us at www.ablongman.com

ISBN 0-321-27614-0

7 8 9 10 V036 10

Contents

Editor's Introduction

A recent article in *Newsweek* explains how young Islamic radicals in Britain appeal to John Stuart Mill's arguments in *On Liberty* to defend their right to express their extremist views.[1] Another article, this one in *The Economist*, considers whether or not "soft paternalism," which involves subtle, often unobtrusive measures to alter people's behavior for the better, is consistent with Mill's outlook in *On Liberty*.[2] One example of such a measure is a scheme by the state of Missouri that allows compulsive gamblers to voluntarily add their names to a list of individuals who are forbidden, under penalty of law, from entering riverboat casinos. Another example is the growing trend of companies signing up employees for pension or 401k plans by default, rather than requiring employees themselves to take the initiative to sign up. A quick search of the popular media, blogs, and academic literature finds pundits, ordinary citizens, and scholars alike struggling to understand the implications of Mill's views for the most controversial issues of the day. The arguments of *On Liberty* surface in the current debates over flag burning, same-sex marriage, the legalization of drugs, smoking bans, hate speech codes and laws, the censorship of pornography, and motorcycle helmet and seatbelt laws. Mill's essay is the starting point for a great deal of political discussion in our society.

On Liberty presents a powerful defense of individual freedom. At its core is Mill's claim—known today as the Harm Principle—that the use of legal and social coercion is justified only to the extent that it prevents harm to other people. In short, people should be free to think, say, and do as they please, so long as it harms no one but themselves. This implies that paternalism (restricting an individual's freedom for his or her own good) is not legitimate. Mill wrote that:

> The "Liberty" is likely to survive longer than anything else that I
> have written ... because ... it is a kind of philosophic text-book of a
> single truth, which the changes progressively taking place in mod-
> ern society tend to bring out into even stronger relief: the impor-
> tance, to man and society, of a large variety in types of character,
> and of giving full freedom to human nature to expand itself in
> innumerable and conflicting directions.[3]

Although the conclusions and arguments of *On Liberty* are of lasting
importance, they were shaped by the historical context in which Mill
thought and wrote. He was deeply disturbed by the stifling morality and
the tendency towards conformity that characterized the Victorian Age in
which he lived. Most of his contemporaries, Mill thought, lived their
lives, not as they themselves saw fit, but according to the customs of society and the expectations of others. Of course, many of these moral
norms and customs were reinforced by legal sanctions. Mill was convinced that individual and social progress could never occur in such a
repressive environment. Human advancement and improvement will
occur only where individuals are free to live their lives as they themselves
choose (so long as they harm no one else in doing this, of course).

On Liberty was recognized as a classic immediately upon its publication. Mill's analysis continues to be relevant for several reasons. Two of
these are related to the nature of modern, liberal-democratic societies.
First, there is an ongoing debate in liberal societies about the proper
scope of government. By "liberal society" is intended a society, like the
United States or the United Kingdom, that attaches great significance to
individual liberty or freedom. Liberals demand a substantial realm of
personal freedom that should be immune from government intrusion.[4]
But determining the precise boundaries of the government's power is difficult. A second factor involves the pluralism or multiculturalism that
increasingly characterizes liberal societies. The citizens of these societies
have different, often sharply conflicting understandings about what is
good and bad, right and wrong, and, ultimately, the meaning of life.
Many of the public policy debates mentioned a moment ago, such as the
dispute over same-sex marriage, make manifest these fundamental dis-
agreements. This raises some very difficult questions about what stance
the government should take with respect to these competing viewpoints.
Should the government remain neutral, or should it promote a common
morality through legislation and policy? What norms should govern the
expression of these viewpoints, particularly when some people find them

very offensive? Mill addresses all of these fundamental issues, which we still grapple with today, head-on in *On Liberty*.

But it is not merely the fact that Mill addresses questions that continue to be of interest to us that explains *On Liberty's* staying power. Many people are attracted by the *method* that Mill employs in his analysis. He defends individual freedom in terms of its utility. That is, he weighs the costs and benefits of adopting alternative principles and policies, and endorses those that maximize the benefits for all. This utilitarian approach to political morality is very attractive. It is a secular approach and does not rest upon any suspect theological or metaphysical assumptions. Moreover, it reflects a naturalistic or scientific approach to questions of political morality, analyzing alternative courses of action in terms of their empirical consequences. Utilitarianism also reflects a basic principle of rationality—a better state of affairs is always preferable to a worse state of affairs. Perhaps it goes without saying, but a final reason for Mill's persistent influence is that a great many people simply think that he is right, and those who do not, nonetheless recognize the power of his arguments and feel compelled to address them.

The following introduction contains four sections. The first section provides a sketch of Mill's biography and the historical context that gave shape to *On Liberty*. The second section takes up utilitarianism, the normative theory in terms of which Mill defends liberty. The third section provides a synopsis of the essay, explaining the main themes and arguments of each chapter. The introduction concludes with a discussion of some of the main interpretive and critical issues raised by Mill's essay.

JOHN STUART MILL'S
LIFE AND TIMES

When John Stuart Mill was 47 he believed that he was soon going to die of consumption. Understandably, this created a great sense of urgency. He felt as though he had much to say, but little time left to say it. So he composed a draft of his autobiography in which he provided an account of his intellectual development and sketched out his views on various subjects that he feared he would not live to fully address. Fortunately, Mill lived for another twenty years and wrote the works that he planned. *On Liberty* is among these. His *Autobiography*, which he revised and updated later in his life, provides us with rare insight into the development of a great philosophical mind.

When Mill looked back upon his life, he saw it through the lens of his mature views, and he interpreted the facts of his life in terms of these views. He intended his autobiography to serve as an example of the progressive self-development that he thought was central to human happiness. He also intended it to illustrate his view that, though an individual's character is determined by his circumstances, the individual has the ability to change his character by changing his circumstances. The work also demonstrates the importance for self-development of opening oneself to diverse influences. Self-development, Mill thought, presupposes a willingness to learn from others—a willingness to seek out truth in opinions that conflict with one's own. Mill's *Autobiography* is invaluable then not only as an historical account of his life, but also as a dramatic, extended example of some the most important themes in his philosophy, many of which are developed in *On Liberty*.

Mill clearly regarded himself as a man of his times, and he recognized that his times involved significant social, political, and economic transition. Concerning one of his primary motives for writing his autobiography, he says,

> It...seemed to me that in an age of transition in opinions, there may be somewhat both of interest and of benefit in noting the successive phases of any mind which was always pressing forward, equally ready to learn and to unlearn either from its own thoughts or from those of others.[5]

Today historians describe this "age of transition" as a period of rapid modernization, characterized by the expansion of democracy, industrialization, commercialization, and mass communication. Bringing about such a modern society was broadly the goal of the Enlightenment thinkers of the 18th century. But many others regarded this vision of society to be extremely unattractive, and a variety of intellectual reactions to Enlightenment ideals, such as Romanticism, appeared in the early-19th century. "The fight between the nineteenth century and the eighteenth," Mill tells us, "always reminded me of the battle about the shield, one side of which was white and the other black."[6] Mill is alluding to a medieval allegory in which two knights ride up from opposite directions to a shield hanging from a tree. One side of the shield is white and the other black. The two knights argue and then fight about the color of the shield—each having seen only one side of it—until a third knight rides up and points out the difference between the two sides. Mill saw himself as the third knight in the intellectual battle between the thinkers of the 18th and 19th centuries. Each side had grasped a "half-truth," and Mill intended to resolve the battle by bringing together the insights of both sides. Let's now consider some of the details of Mill's biography, bearing in mind his own insistence that we see his life as embodying the era of transition in which he lived.[7]

John Stuart Mill was born in the London suburb of Pentonville on May 20, 1806, the eldest child of James and Harriet Mill. James Mill (1773-1836) was a leading intellectual figure in his own day.[8] Born of humble origin in the small Scottish town of Northwater Bridge, James attended Edinburgh University thanks to the patronage of a member of the local gentry—Sir John Stuart, for whom James named his son. After a half-hearted attempt to make a career in the clergy, James made his way to London in 1802 to live as a writer. He married Harriet Burrow in 1805, and at about this same time he undertook his first major work, the *History of British India* (1817-18). This work secured James a permanent position at the East India Company, which essentially ran the Indian subcontinent until the British government took over direct control of the region in 1858. James eventually became the senior civil servant in the company's London office.

Today James Mill is best known as the leading disciple of Jeremy Bentham (1748-1832).[9] Mill met Bentham in 1808 and soon became his chief companion and assistant. Together Mill and Bentham championed the principle of utility, or the greatest happiness principle, as the standard against which all human conduct is to be evaluated. This principle tells us that in all of our actions we should strive to bring about the greatest happiness for the greatest number of people, where happiness is understood to come from pleasurable experiences. In his theoretical writings James Mill explored the foundations of the principle of utility and applied it in a wide variety of contexts. His *Essay on Government* (1820) presents the utilitarian case for representative democracy, and his *Elements of Political Economy* (1821) became a standard textbook on the free-trade economics of his close friend David Ricardo (1772-1823). Mill claimed to have made the operations of the human mind "as plain as the road from St. Paul's to Charing Cross" in his *Analysis of the Phenomena of the Human Mind* (1829). In this work he grounds utilitarianism in the associationist psychology of John Locke (1632-1704) and David Hartley (1705-1757).

These works provided the theoretical foundation for the democratic and humane political reform advocated by the Philosophical Radicals, a loose-knit group of public intellectuals and politicians whose ranks included the economist Ricardo, the classical historian George Grote (1794-1871), the population control advocate Francis Place (1771-1854), and the legal theorist John Austin (1790-1859).[10] The Radicals thought the political implications of utilitarianism to be straightforward: the end of government is to eliminate pain and suffering and to create conditions under which citizens can pursue happiness. Social evils, the Radicals thought, result primarily from the ignorance of the general population and the government's nefarious pursuit of special interests at the expense of the common good.[11] These obstacles to happiness were to be eliminated through the implementation of universal education and a representative form of democracy. From our vantage point today it is perhaps difficult to see this as radical doctrine. But as Bentham reported with considerable delight in his *Principles of Morals and Legislation* (1789), the aristocrats of his day saw utilitarianism as a very dangerous doctrine.

John Mill's *Autobiography* describes in detail the extraordinary education that he received from his father with the advice and assistance of Bentham. The overt goal of this education, his father wrote in a letter to Bentham, was to "leave [John] a successor worthy of both of us."[12] John was learning Greek at three and Latin at eight. By the time that he reached his early-teens, he was thoroughly versed in economics, history, logic, mathematics, natural science, law, and philosophy. He was made responsible for the education of his younger siblings and served as a secretary to his father. He read the proofs of his father's *History*, aided in the composition of the *Elements*, and acted as a sounding board as his father developed the arguments of the *Analysis*. Isolated from other children his age, John kept the same company as his father. His education was capped at fourteen with a year's stay in France at the home of Jeremy Bentham's brother, Sir Samuel Bentham. There John studied the language and developed what would become a life-long interest in French culture. Upon his return to England, John was presented with a copy of Étienne Dumont's French redaction of Bentham's *Traité de Législation* (1802). Mill describes his response to the work:

> When I laid down the last volume of the *Traité* I had become a different being. The "principle of utility" understood as Bentham understood it, and applied in the manner in which he applied it through these three volumes, fell exactly into its place as the keystone which held together the detached and fragmentary component parts of my knowledge and beliefs. It gave unity to my

conceptions of things. I now had opinions; a creed, a doctrine, a philosophy; in one among the best senses of the word, a religion; the inculcation and diffusion of which could be made the principal outward purpose of a life. And I had a grand conception laid before me of changes to be effected in the condition of mankind through that doctrine.[13]

Mill now entered a period of "youthful propagandism," and with missionary zeal he set out to reform the world according to the tenets of his "religion" of utilitarianism. He sought new converts through the Utilitarian Society, which he founded at 16, and he wrote prodigiously for newspapers and periodicals, including the *Westminster Review* which Bentham founded in 1824 to serve as the official organ for the utilitarian movement. Mill campaigned on behalf of all of the typical utilitarian causes: parliamentary reform, improvements to the civil and criminal law, wider suffrage, a free-market, a free press, the abolition of slavery, population control, and a remedy for Irish grievances. He also defended the utilitarian platform in the London Debating Society. The young radical even took to the streets and on one occasion was arrested and jailed for promoting the use of contraceptives. During this period John strongly identified with the French *philosophes* of the 18th century—figures like Voltaire (1694-1778) and Diderot (1713-84) whose withering critiques of the *ancien régime* led to its overthrow in the Revolution. At this time John also settled on a career. His father arranged a position for him in the East India Company in 1823, and John would work at India House for the next 35 years.

It would seem that James Mill had succeeded in creating the standard-bearer for the next generation of Benthamite utilitarians. But in 1826, at the age of 20, John Stuart Mill suffered a mental crisis—a prolonged depression—that led him to question his faith in Bentham's creed. He tells us:

From the winter of 1821, when I first read Bentham, and especially from the commencement of the *Westminster Review*, I had what might truly be called an object in life; to be a reformer of the world....But the time came when I awakened from this as from a dream. It was in the autumn of 1826....it occurred to me to put the question directly to myself, "Suppose that all your objects in life were realized; that all the changes in institutions and opinions which you are looking to forward to, could be completely effected at this very instant: would this be a great joy and happiness to

you?" And an irrepressible self-consciousness distinctly answered,
"No!" At this my heart sank within me: the whole foundation on
which my life was constructed fell down.[14]

At the core of Mill's crisis was the sense that his education had been
grossly deficient in certain areas. While his intellect had been honed to a
razor's edge, his emotional development had been entirely disregarded.
His father, Mill tells us, "professed the greatest contempt" for passionate
emotions; indeed, he "regarded them as a form of madness."[15] Mill
feared that his education had left him a mere reasoning machine, without
the ability to feel at all. So he was greatly relieved when a passage in
Jean-François Marmontel's *Mémoires d'un père* (1804) reduced him to
tears, confirming that his capacity to feel had not been wholly eradi-
cated.[16] Mill now undertook a second, self-directed education, in which
the cultivation of his feelings was central. He found an immediate anti-
dote for his depression in the poetry of William Wordsworth (1770-
1850).[17] Mill tells us that Wordsworth's poems, which evoke strong
emotional responses through the vivid portrayal of natural beauty,
"seemed to be the very culture of the feelings, which I was in quest of."[18]
Poetry, Mill came to believe, is capable of revealing certain truths even
better than philosophy.

Mill's crisis confirmed in the most direct way that his father and Bentham did not have an adequate grasp of human nature, and, hence, the
opinions that he had inherited from them needed to be critically evaluated. He now opened himself to a wide variety of intellectual influences
and sought to thoroughly understand the views opposed to those of the
classical utilitarians. He identifies the most important of these opposing
views for us:

> The influences of European, that is to say Continental, thought,
> and especially those of the reaction in the nineteenth century
> against the eighteenth, were now streaming in upon me. They came
> from various quarters: from the writings of Coleridge [the English
> poet, critic, and philosopher Samuel Taylor Coleridge (1772-
> 1834)—ed.], which I had begun to read with interest even before
> the change of my opinions; from the Coleridgians with whom I was
> in personal intercourse [for example, the author John Sterling
> (1806-44) and the theologian F.D. Maurice (1805-72)—ed.]; from
> what I had read of Goethe [the German poet and dramatist Johann
> Wolfgang von Goethe (1749-1832)—ed.]; from Carlyle's [the
> British historian and essayist Thomas Carlyle (1795-1881)—ed.]

early articles in the *Edinburgh* and *Foreign* Reviews....The writers from whom, more than by any others, a new mode of political thinking was brought home to me, were those of the St. Simonian school in France [the school associated with the French social theorist and founder of Christian socialism Claude Henri de Rouvroy, comte de Saint-Simon (1760-1825)—ed.].[19]

Mill found a number of insights in these sources. He came to believe that political institutions and principles are historically conditioned and, therefore, a political philosophy presupposes a theory of human progress—that is, a philosophy of history. He came to see that "all questions of political institutions are relative, not absolute, and that different stages of human progress not only *will* have, but *ought* to have, different institutions."[20] So, the political philosopher must understand the broader historical and social context before making prescriptions. As Mill indicates, his own understanding of human history was largely shaped by the Saint-Simonians. Mill accepted their view that human history alternates between "organic" and "critical" periods. During organic periods society accepts some comprehensive doctrine as an authoritative guide to life, and, consequently, these periods are characterized by social cohesion, stability, and steady progress. But over time conditions change and the comprehensive doctrine comes to be seen as an obstacle to further progress. A critical period arises during which the old doctrine is deposed and a new doctrine ascends. Predictably, these critical periods are characterized by considerable social unrest and instability. Mill saw his age as a critical one, and his philosophical program was largely determined by this perception. The function of a philosopher during such times is to lead society to a new doctrine that is capable of attracting the widespread appeal needed to usher in a new organic period, before the forces of instability get the better of society and it disintegrates.

Coleridge, too, emphasized the importance of analyzing social and political institutions in their historical context. He insisted that the institutions of previous ages, no matter how archaic they may seem from our contemporary point of view, served some purpose in their time. So in evaluating these institutions one must look beyond their external trappings and try to appreciate the fundamental role that these institutions play in society. Coleridge's discussion of a "clerisy" convinced Mill of the persistent need for an elite, learned class to guide social opinion. Carlyle's writings, which Mill tended to value as much for their rhetorical force as for their content, reinforced the view that a common, authoritative doctrine is needed to preserve social stability. Together Coleridge and Carlyle persuaded Mill that there is some truth to be found in certain tenets of conservative political philosophy. Mill came to believe that efforts to reform society must be balanced by concerns for social stability, and, moreover, that traditional institutions and a cultured class play a very important role in fostering and maintaining this stability.

These sources not only played a significant role in shaping Mill's philosophical program, they also provided him with a framework for analyzing the place of his father and Bentham in the history of ideas. The Benthamite utilitarians, he thought, played a vital role in destroying the comprehensive doctrine associated with monarchy, a landed aristocracy, and a feudal economy. But the tasks of a critical age are not just destructive, they are also constructive; and Mill came to think that Bentham's utilitarianism could not provide the foundation for a new organic age. His reflections upon his father at his death in 1836 are instructive:

> As Brutus was called the last of the Romans, so was he the last of the eighteenth century: he continued its tone of thought and sentiment into the nineteenth (though not unmodified nor unimproved), partaking neither in the good nor bad influences of the reaction against the eighteenth century, which was the great characteristic of the first half of the nineteenth. The eighteenth century was a great age, an age of strong and brave men, and he was a fit companion for the strongest and bravest.[21]

The task of the 18th century was the destruction of the old social, political, and economic order, and Bentham's utilitarianism was well-suited for this task. The task of the 19th century, however, was to construct a new order, and here Bentham's utilitarianism was not up to the task.

This is because Bentham's utilitarianism rested on an impoverished understanding of human nature and, consequently, a deficient account of human happiness. Bentham failed to recognize the wide-range of motives and feelings that drive human conduct. In particular he failed to recognize the human desire for perfection—the desire to improve one's self and to realize what is best in one's nature. Moreover, Bentham failed to recognize the variability of human nature, and, hence, he also failed to recognize the value of individuality. Both of these points were brought home to Mill by the German Romantics, often indirectly through Coleridge and Carlyle, but also directly through Goethe. Bentham supposed that the end of life is simple contentment, achieved through the satisfaction of relatively fixed wants and desires. This was not, to Mill's mind, a progressive doctrine. He found the Romantic's notion of *Bildung*—a process of self-development or self-culture that involves critically evaluating, refining, and improving one's wants and desires—much more attractive, and he came to believe that such self-development is essential to human happiness. These sources led Mill to question not only the *content* of his father and Bentham's utilitarianism, but also their decidedly ahistorical, deductive *methodology* in political philosophy. In his *Essay on Government* the senior Mill attempted to formally deduce universal principles of political philosophy—principles of government true for all societies at all times—from a few fundamental truths about human nature. This approach is squarely at odds with the historicism of the Saint-Simonians and conservatives, who emphasized that political institutions and principles must be adapted to the broader historical and social context. Mill's sense that his father's methods in political philosophy were deficient was reinforced by Thomas Macauly's (1800-1859) caustic review of the *Essay* that was published in the *Edinburgh Review* in 1829.

Recognizing the deficiencies of Bentham's utilitarianism did not lead Mill to a wholesale repudiation of the doctrine; rather, he sought to amend utilitarianism in light of what he found valuable in other views. "I found the fabric of my old and taught opinions giving way in many fresh places," he remembers, "and I never allowed it to fall to pieces, but was incessantly occupied in weaving it anew."[22] While Bentham's utilitarianism could not serve as a comprehensive doctrine for a new organic age, Mill believed that a more humane form of utilitarianism could. In the following section we will consider precisely how Mill modified Bentham's utilitarianism in order to accommodate the insights that he found in others' views.

Now convinced that "the true system [of political philosophy] was something much more complex and many sided than [he] had previously had any idea of,"[23] Mill abandoned his doctrinaire approach to social and political philosophy in favor of "eclecticism" or "many-sidedness"—the latter a term he claims to have found in Goethe. He would pursue truth wherever he found it and avoid ideology. Mill's eclecticism is evident in a number of essays and occasional pieces that he published in the 1830s, including "Spirit of the Age" (1831), "Civilization" (1836), "On Bentham" (1838), and "On Coleridge" (1840). In these writings we find Mill playing the role of the third knight, attempting to resolve the battle between the utilitarians and their opponents by showing each side the "half-truths" that the other side had grasped. Mill maintained his association with the Radicals through the 1830s, but they ultimately did not welcome his revisions to utilitarianism and regarded his pointed critique of Bentham as treasonous.

Another important influence on Mill's intellectual development during the 1830s was Alexis de Tocqueville (1805-59). Like all British radicals, and European liberals more generally, Mill was profoundly interested in the development of democracy in the United States. Tocqueville was sent to the United States by the French government to study the American prison system in 1831. He spent nine months traveling around the United States, taking notes on all aspects of American society. Tocqueville's comprehensive analysis of American political culture, *De la Démocratie en Amerique* (*Democracy in America*, 2 vols. 1835, 1840), was hailed as a groundbreaking work of political science and sociology. Mill wrote reviews of both volumes of *Democracy*, and the work had a profound impact on his political thought. It was particularly important in defining the fundamental problem addressed in *On Liberty*. Although he did find faults with the work—for example, Tocqueville had failed to define the work's key concept, democracy, with precision, and, hence, he sometimes confused the effects of *democracy* with the effects of *commercial society* more generally—Mill held the work in high esteem. Tocqueville, more than any of his other contemporaries, recognized both the advantages and disadvantages that attend democratic culture.

Tocqueville and Mill had both come to see the expansion of democracy as the inevitable result of human progress. So they were not encouraged to find that democracy involves perennial threats to freedom of thought and discussion and to individuality. Tocqueville makes these dangers clear in the following passages from Volume I, Chapter XV, entitled "Unlimited Power of the Majority in the United States, and Its Consequences":

It is in the examination of the exercise of thought in the United States that we clearly perceive how far the power of the majority surpasses all the powers with which we are acquainted in Europe. Thought is an invisible and subtle power that mocks all the efforts of tyranny. At the present time the most absolute monarchs in Europe cannot prevent certain opinions hostile to their authority from circulating in secret through their dominions and even in their courts. It is not so in America; as long as the majority is still undecided, discussion is carried on; but as soon as its decision is irrevocably pronounced, everyone is silent, and the friends as well as the opponents of the measure unite in assenting to its propriety. The reason for this is perfectly clear: no monarch is so absolute as to combine all the powers of society into his own hands and to conquer all opposition, as a majority is able to do, which has the right both of making and of executing the laws.

The authority of a king is physical and controls the actions of men without subduing their will. But the majority possesses a power that is physical and moral at the same time, which acts upon the will as much as upon the actions and represses not only all contest, but all controversy.

I know of no country in which there is so little independence of mind and real freedom of discussion as in America....In America the majority raises formidable barriers around the liberty of opinion; within these barriers an author may write what he pleases, but woe to him if he goes beyond them....In that immense crowd which throngs the avenues to power in the United States, I found very few men who displayed that manly candor and masculine independence of opinion which frequently distinguished the Americans in former times, and which constitutes the leading feature in distinguished characters wherever they may be found. It seems at first sight as if all the minds of the Americans were formed upon one model, so accurately do they follow the same route.[24]

For James Mill the fundamental problem of political philosophy involved the antagonism between the interests of the sovereign and the people. This antagonism, he thought, was overcome in a democratic society where the people themselves *are* sovereign. He regarded it as a logical truth that in a democracy the sovereign cannot have interests opposed to those of the people, and, therefore, a democratic society is immune to tyranny. But, of course, making *the people* sovereign really amounts to making *the majority* of people sovereign, and a majority certainly *can* have interests opposed to those of a minority. The threat of political tyranny is real even in a democracy. What is more, Tocqueville discovered that the people of the United States had internalized the democratic principle of political legitimacy—majority rule—and venerated the opinion of the majority in general. If the opinion of the majority is recognized as authoritative in *political* matters, then, the Americans seemed to have collectively reasoned, there must be something special about the opinion of the majority *in general*. And if this is so, then the opinion of the majority must be regarded as authoritative in *all* matters. So, once the opinion of the majority is expressed, Tocqueville found, Americans feel a deep compulsion to conform to it both in their behavior and thought. To the extent that the Americans *want* to act and think according to the expectations of the majority, the majority in the new American democracy exercises a power far more tyrannical than that of any European monarch.

By 1840 the fundamental revolution in Mill's thinking was complete, and in the next decade he published two works that secured his reputation—*A System of Logic* (1843) and *The Principles of Political Economy* (1848). Both works quickly became standard texts in their respective fields and remained in use well into the late-19th century. The *Logic* is primarily a work on inferential knowledge—knowledge acquired through deduction or induction—but Mill thought that its conclusions were of great practical importance, and it is worth considering some of its main themes here. The *Logic* defends empiricism (the view that all human knowledge derives either from direct experience or reasoning upon experience) and offers a thoroughgoing critique of intuitionism (the view that some knowledge is directly apprehended without recourse to sense experience). Intuitionism seems most plausible in logic and mathematics, since the fundamental truths of these disciplines seem to be self-evident and their denial seems to be inconceivable. But many intuitionists contend that knowledge in other disciplines, including science and ethics, is also known by intuition. In ethics intuitionism involves the claim that we directly perceive non-natural moral properties (goodness or rightness) through a "moral sense."[25] According to the intuitionist, beliefs arising from intuition are directly justified, and do not need to be justified by appeal to other beliefs. Intuitionism, Mill thought, is not only bad epistemology, it is dangerous.

> The notion that truths external to the mind may be known by intuition or consciousness, independently of observation and experience, is, I am persuaded, in these times, the great intellectual support of false doctrines and bad institutions. By the aid of this theory, every inveterate belief and every intense feeling, of which the origin is not remembered, is enabled to dispense with the obligation of justifying itself by reason, and is erected into its own all-sufficient voucher and justification. There never was such an instrument devised for consecrating all deep seated prejudices. And the chief strength of this false philosophy in morals, politics and

religion, lies in the appeal which it is accustomed to make to the evidence of mathematics and of the cognate branches of physical science. To expel it from these, is to drive it from its stronghold....[26]

Mill saw a very clear connection between intuitionism and conservative moral and political philosophy. He had already attacked moral intuitionism specifically in a number of essays,[27] but by arguing in the *Logic* that logic and mathematics themselves rest upon empirical foundations, Mill sought to overthrow intuitionism altogether by assailing it in the very disciplines where it seemed most secure. Mill ridicules moral intuitionism in several places in the opening chapter of *On Liberty*.

Another aim of the *Logic* was to extend the empirical methods of natural science into the so-called "moral sciences"—what we today call the social sciences. After David Hume (1711-76) many people thought of empiricism as a skeptical and critical doctrine. Mill sought to show that empiricism could, and should, serve as the foundation for constructive thinking not only in the natural sciences but also in political and social matters. Mill proposed a science of character, which he called "ethology," that would explain character formation and actions resulting from various character-types. Establishing such a science would be the first step in developing a broader sociology that would explain human interactions in a scientific manner. But while Mill was excited by the prospect of bringing human affairs under the guidance of science, he also saw a troubling implication. If human actions, like all other actions in nature, are causally determined by prior events and natural laws and are therefore open to scientific analysis, how can the individual be free to form his or her own character? This problem had troubled Mill for some time. At the time of his mental crisis Mill was deeply worried that his father's education had left him a "manufactured man." He writes,

the doctrine of what is called Philosophical Necessity weighed on my existence like an incubus. I felt as if I was scientifically proved to be the helpless slave of antecedent circumstances; as if the character of all persons had been formed for them by agencies beyond our truth...[28]

The doctrine of philosophical necessity—what today is called determinism—seems to undermine the very notion of self-development, and, for that matter, the notion of social reform. Mill's solution to this problem was to concede that character is the product of circumstances, but to insist that our desire to change our character is itself casually efficacious and can lead us to put ourselves in circumstances that will, over time, change our character, thereby changing the way we act. Of course, the natural question here is, what gives rise to the desire to change our character in the first place? Mill does not answer this question, but takes his own change our character to provide evidence for the view.

Along with his father and Bentham, another individual who exerted a tremendous influence on Mill's thought and life was Harriet Taylor (1807-58).[29] The two were introduced in 1830, when he was 24 and she was 23. Harriet was the wife of a wealthy London merchant, John Taylor, and the mother of two. She was intellectually able—Mill would say that relative to himself and Carlyle, Harriet was "the superior of us both...more a poet than he, and more a thinker than I"[30]—and she desired intellectual companionship and respect beyond what her husband was willing or able to provide. The two soon fell in love, but out of concern for her husband and children Harriet refused to seek a divorce. Instead, she brokered an arrangement that proved suitable to all parties. She maintained a residence separate from her husband where Mill was free to visit her, and, though she and Mill never went out in society as a couple, the two frequently traveled abroad together. The relationship was carried out in this form for 20 years, and though all evidence suggests that the relationship was purely Platonic, it was regarded as scandalous in Victorian England. John and Harriet suffered the disapproval of friends and family members.[31] If his reading of Tocqueville provoked abstract anxieties about the stifling effects of middle-class sensibilities, the disapprobation directed towards the couple certainly made these lessons concrete.

John Taylor died in 1849. After what Harriet deemed an appropriate interval—two years—and after writing out a formal renunciation of the English marriage contract, John Stuart and Harriet were married. But the marriage was to be short-lived. John and Harriet had contracted tuberculosis. He most likely contracted it from his father and infected Harriet in turn. The two regarded death as a threat not only to their personal relationship but also to their intellectual legacy. Together they planned a series of short essays that would express their views on a variety of subjects and, as Mill put it in a letter to Harriet, would serve as "a sort of mental pemmican for thinkers—if there are any—who come after us."[32] These essays were to be published together in a single volume prefaced by Mill's autobiography, which, in addition to its other purposes, would offer a vindication of their personal relationship. The essays were drafted as the two journeyed across Europe in search of healthier climes. But as

Mill's condition improved, Harriet's deteriorated. She died in Avignon, France seven years after their marriage. Mill bought a small cottage next to the cemetery where she was buried, and he spent part of every year there for the rest of his life. *On Liberty* was the only essay that was complete at the time of Harriet's death, and, as the work's dedication indicates (see p. 61), it was published as a memorial to her.

Mill would claim that his intellectual debt to Harriet was "almost infinite," and that his best writings "were as much her work as mine."[33] The following passages from Mill's *Autobiography* describe both the circumstances in which *On Liberty* was conceived and Harriet's influence upon the composition of the work:

> During the two years which immediately preceded the cessation of my official life, my wife and I were working at the *Liberty*. I had first planned and written it as a short essay, in 1854. It was in mounting the steps of the Capitol [in Rome], in January, 1855, that the thought first arose of converting it into a volume. None of my writings have been either so carefully composed, or so sedulously corrected as this. After it had been written as usual twice over, we kept it by us, bringing it out from time to time and going through it *de novo*, reading, weighing and criticizing every sentence. Its final revision was to have been a work of the winter of 1858/59, the first after my retirement, which we had arranged to pass in the South of Europe. That hope and every other were frustrated by the most unexpected and bitter calamity of her death—at Avignon, on our way to Montpelier, from a sudden attack of pulmonary congestion....
>
> The *Liberty* was more directly and more literally our joint production than anything else which bears my name, for there was not a sentence of it that was not several times gone through by us together, turned over in many ways, and carefully weeded of any faults, either in thought or expression, that we detected in it. It is in consequence of this that, although it never underwent her final revision, it far surpasses, as a mere specimen of composition, anything which has proceeded from me either before or since. With regard to the thoughts, it is difficult to identify any particular part or element as being more hers than all the rest. The whole mode of thinking of which the book was the expression, was emphatically hers. But I also was so thoroughly imbued with it that the same thoughts naturally occurred to us both. That I was thus penetrated

with it, however, I owe a great degree to her. There was a moment in my mental progress when I might easily have fallen into a tendency toward over-government, both social and political; as there was also a moment when, by reaction from a contrary excess, I might have become a less thorough radical and democrat than I am. In both these points as in many others, she benefited me as much by keeping me where I was right, as by leading me to new truths and ridding me of errors.[34]

The true extent of Harriet's influence upon Mill's thought has been the subject of much debate. While some take his claim that his later works were their joint productions at face value, many other commentators see Mill's praise of Harriet as so effusive that it simply cannot be regarded as realistic.[35]

Mill assumed the position of Chief Examiner of India Correspondence in 1856, and in the following year he composed the petition requesting the renewal of the Company's charter. When the petition was denied and the British government assumed direct control of India, Mill declined a position on the government's India Council and retired. As Mill indicated in the passages from the *Autobiography* cited above, his hopes to spend his retirement in quiet contemplation with Harriet were dashed. After his wife's death Mill completed and published the works for which he is best known today. He published a series of articles on moral philosophy in *Fraser's Magazine* in the fall of 1861. These articles were reprinted together in 1863 as *Utilitarianism*. We will consider the main themes of this work in some detail in the following section. *Considerations on Representative Government* (1861) defends representative democracy on the grounds that it, better than any other form of government, leads to the progressive development of the mental and moral faculties of those who practice it. *An Examination of Sir William Hamilton's Philosophy* (1865) is an all-out attack on intuitionism, and *Auguste Comte and Positivism* (1865) assesses the thought of the influential French Sociologist. *The Subjection of Women* (1869), which perhaps owes a greater debt to Harriet than any of his works, is one of the foundational documents of modern feminism. Here Mill shows that the social, political, and economic inequalities between men and women do not rest upon natural differences between the sexes, but are wholly the product of artifice.

In 1865 Mill was persuaded to stand as parliamentary candidate for Westminster. As a Liberal MP he fought for extending suffrage to the working class and women, the rights of worker's to organize, Irish land reform, and a second reform bill. He was a leader of the Jamaica Committee, which investigated the actions of Governor Edward Eyre in the aftermath of the Jamaica Mutiny (1865). After losing his seat in the 1868 election, Mill spent most of his time in Avignon, where he lived with his stepdaughter Helen Taylor in a small house near Harriet's grave. He died at Avignon on May 8, 1873. His *Autobiography*, edited by Helen Taylor, was published later the same year. Two additional works—*Three Essays on Religion* (1874) and *Chapters on Socialism* (1879)—were published posthumously.

Commentators disagree about whether Mill's attempt to bring together the ideals of the 18th century with those of the 19th century was successful—or even possible, for that matter. Traditionally, many commentators claimed to find no consistent doctrine in Mill's self-confessedly eclectic thought.[36] His thinking, they argued, vacillates and is plagued by contradictions. The incoherence of Mill's philosophical program is clearly manifest in *On Liberty's* attempt to offer a utilitarian justification for liberty, which these traditional commentators saw as an attempt to square the circle. More recent scholars have seen in Mill a coherent and systematic philosophical program, while still acknowledging defects in that program.[37] The following section considers Mill's attempt to reconcile his utilitarian inheritance with the Romantic notion of self-development.

UTILITARIANISM

Mill defends individual liberty on the grounds of its utility. In the essay's opening chapter he tells us,

> It is proper to state that I forego any advantage which could be derived to my argument from the idea of abstract right as a thing independent of utility. I regard utility as the ultimate appeal on all ethical questions; but it must be utility in the largest sense, grounded on the permanent interests of man as a progressive being. (71)

Mill supposes that his reader is already acquainted with utilitarianism, so it is appropriate that we should familiarize ourselves with that doctrine. Although strains of utilitarian thought appear throughout the history of ethics, Jeremy Bentham offered the first systematic account of the theory.

Here we will approach Mill's utilitarianism by way of considering his attempt to improve upon Bentham's account. Let's start with a very rough sketch of utilitarianism.

Utilitarianism is a form of *consequentialism*. It holds that actions (or decisions or policies) are morally right or wrong solely in virtue of their consequences—that is, in virtue of the good or bad that they bring about. Non-consequentialist approaches to morality, by contrast, claim that certain kinds of actions are morally right or wrong *in themselves*, independent of their consequences. The German philosopher Immanuel Kant (1724-1804), for example, argued that lying is wrong in itself and, hence, it is always our duty to tell the truth. The utilitarian, though, claims that lying is wrong—when it is wrong—only because the consequences of lying are, on balance, bad. It is possible that on certain occasions the consequences of lying will be, on balance, better than the consequences of telling the truth, and on these occasions it is right that we should lie. So, for the utilitarian, moral *goodness* is more fundamental than or prior to moral *rightness*. In order to understand utilitarianism's fundamental injunction—"maximize the general good"—we must first understand what 'good' means. Utilitarians speak alternatively of 'good,' 'utility,' and 'happiness,' but what is intended by all of these terms is the notion of intrinsic value (that which is valuable for its own sake, and not merely as a means to some further end). Money is a good, but it is typically regarded as an extrinsic good. Except in the odd case of misers, we do not value money for its own sake; we value it because of the other things that we can get with it. The classical utilitarians identified happiness with the experience of pleasure. The view that the sole intrinsic good is pleasure and the sole intrinsic bad is pain is known as *hedonism*. But there can be as many varieties of utilitarianism as there are conceptions of intrinsic value. Two utilitarians may agree that morality is fundamentally about maximizing good, but disagree about the nature of goodness.

Utilitarianism is attractive for several reasons. It allows us to think about morality in a systematic and rational way by grounding our moral thinking in one fundamental principle. But what is more, this fundamental principle reflects what seems to be a basic principle of rationality—a better state of affairs is always preferable to a worse state of affairs. The aim of morality on a utilitarian approach is simply to bring about the best overall state of affairs possible. Another appealing feature of utilitarianism is its emphasis on the equality of interests. Utilitarianism enjoins us to maximize goodness *in general*, and no one person's or group's interests are <u>privileged over</u> those of another. As Bentham put it, "Each is to count for one, and no one for more than one." This, as we have seen, was a very radical idea in 18th century Britain, where the interests of certain classes were privileged over those of others.

In *An Introduction to the Principles of Morals and Legislation* (1789) Bentham set forth the principle of utility as a guide for legislators. He presents the principle in a famous passage in this work's opening chapter:

> Nature has placed man under the governance of two sovereign masters, *pain* and *pleasure*. It is for them alone to point out what we ought to do, as well as determine what we shall do. On the one hand the standard of right and wrong, on the other the chain of causes and effects, are fastened to their throne....The *principle of utility* recognises this subjection, and assumes it as the foundation of that system....By the principle of utility is meant that principle which approves or disapproves of every action whatsoever, according to the tendency which it appears to have to augment or diminish the happiness of the party whose interest is in question: or, what is the same thing in other words, to promote or oppose that happiness.[38]

The principle of utility, as Bentham frames it, is at once a normative principle (telling us what we *ought* to do) and at the same time a psychological principle (telling us what we *are in fact* motivated to do). At first this may seem confusing: if we are psychologically determined to pursue pleasure and avoid pain, then it trivially follows that we ought to do this. The confusion results from an equivocation in the phrase "the party whose interest is in question." When read as a psychological principle, Bentham intends the phrase to refer to the individual, but when read as a moral and legislative principle, he intends the phrase to refer to society at large. We are, Bentham thinks, in fact motivated primarily by egoistic considerations—a concern for our own personal pleasure. But, if pleasure is intrinsically good, then morally it does not matter whose pleasure is involved, and we ought to strive to maximize pleasure in general. The fact that Bentham casts the principle of utility as both a psychological and a normative principle reflects his desire to give the principle an empirical grounding. As a foundational principle, the principle of utility cannot be proved in terms of other principles. What then justifies the principle? As a fierce opponent to intuitionism, Bentham would never say that the principle is simply self-evident. What he does say is that we are all directly acquainted with pleasure and pain, and, to the extent that we all pursue pleasure as an end in itself, we all acknowledge its intrinsic value.

What then is the nature of the pleasure that we all pursue as the ultimate aim of all of our actions? For Bentham pleasure is an indefinable, irreducible mental state—in general, any agreeable state of consciousness. He maintained that all pleasurable mental states are structurally similar, and, hence, they are all measurable on a single scale. For Bentham then, the only difference between pleasures is *quantitative*—that is, how *much* there is—and the only thing that can make one pleasure superior to another is simply that there is more of it. Given this, Bentham thought that it should be possible to develop a "felicific calculus" that would allow us to calculate the expected utility of alternative actions. For any act that we might perform, we can calculate how many people—or, better, how many sentient beings—will experience pleasure, and for each of these beings we can calculate how intense the pleasure will be, how long it will last, and so forth. When the amount of potential pleasure is multiplied by the probability that the pleasure will actually obtain, we arrive at the act's expected utility. Bentham did think that the pleasures associated with intellectual pursuits tend to be superior to bodily pleasures, since they tend to last longer, tend to offer the prospect of additional pleasure in the future, and tend not to be followed by pain. But, again, he denied that mental pleasures *in themselves* are superior to physical pleasures. As he famously put the point in *The Rationale of Reward*, provided that they generate the same amount of pleasure "the [children's] game of push-pin is of equal value with the arts and sciences of music and poetry."[39]

Bentham's utilitarianism was subject to several common objections. First, critics argued that Bentham's hedonistic psychology is excessively crude and reflects a deeply impoverished understanding of human nature. Humans, the critics argued, properly aspire to higher ideals than the simple pursuit of pleasure. Important among these is the desire to improve oneself. Bentham's theory focuses exclusively upon the character of our *actions*, and says nothing about the character of *individuals*, which is an essential element of morality. Second, critics claimed that Bentham's utilitarianism is not workable in practice, since it is not possible to calculate the expected utility of every possible course of action on every occasion. Finally, critics argued that Bentham's utilitarianism seems to conflict with many of our most deeply held moral beliefs about what is just and right. We can easily imagine cases where sacrificing the well-being of an individual or a minority group would maximize the general good, and would, therefore, be justified on utilitarian grounds.

As we saw in the preceding section, Mill was inclined to believe that these objections contained some truth. Mill's objective was to accommodate the insights of the critics' objections within a utilitarian framework, thereby developing a more inclusive, humane, and progressive doctrine. Mill's own initial statement of utilitarianism strongly echoes Bentham. He writes,

> The creed which accepts as the foundation of morals, Utility, or the Greatest Happiness Principle, holds that actions are right in proportion as they tend to promote happiness, wrong as they tend to produce the reverse of happiness. By happiness is intended pleasure, and the absence of pain; by unhappiness, pain, and the privation of pleasure.[40]

But he immediately adds, "To give a clear view of the moral standard set up by the theory, much more requires to be said; in particular, what things it includes in the ideas of pain and pleasure...."[41] Mill goes on to develop the core concepts of utilitarianism in such a way as to avoid the objections to Bentham's account of the theory; but, in doing this, his own account of utilitarianism departs from Bentham's in important respects.

Coleridge and Carlyle were certainly among the "German, French, and English assailants" of utilitarianism who argued that "[t]o suppose that life has...no higher end than pleasure—no better and nobler object of desire and pursuit—[is] utterly mean and groveling...a doctrine worthy only of swine...."[42] Their point can be made by way of a fanciful example. Consider the life of the philosopher Socrates. His life was devoted to intellectual pursuits and the reform of his home city of Athens, but he was frequently persecuted for his beliefs and activities and was ultimately put to death for them. Some of the most important aims in his life were frustrated. Now consider the life of a very fortunate and extraordinarily long-lived pig. All of this pig's simple needs and desires are fulfilled. Now, if value is simply a matter of the quantity of pleasure, as Bentham's view has it, and if our pig were to live for a *very* long time—far longer than the lifetime of any real pig—then at some point we must agree that the life of the contented pig becomes, on balance, more valuable than the life of the frustrated Socrates, and if we were asked to choose between the two lives, we should prefer that of the contented pig. The critics found this implication of Bentham's view wholly unacceptable. The unlimited satisfaction of our simple animal desires, they insisted, could never compensate us for the loss of our distinctive human capacities. The development of these capacities, in fact, is the true end of human life.

Mill agrees that Bentham's understanding of pleasure, and, hence, his conception of human happiness, is inadequate, but argues that the insights involved in this objection can be accounted for within a utilitarian framework. The utilitarian, Mill argues, can and should take into account not only the *quantity* of pleasure but also its *quality*. He writes,

> It is compatible with the principle of utility to recognize the fact, that some *kinds* of pleasure are more desirable and more valuable than others. It would be absurd that while, in estimating all other things, quality is considered as well as quantity, the estimation of pleasures should be supposed to depend on quantity alone.[43]

A staunch empiricist, Mill maintains that conclusions about which kinds of pleasures are in fact qualitatively superior must be drawn from experience—from a study of actual human choices. But *whose* choices should we study? Who is competent to judge whether one pleasure is qualitatively superior to another? Mill answers, only those who have experienced, and have developed the capacity to appreciate, both pleasures. Moreover, if those who are competent to judge would prefer a smaller quantity of one kind of pleasure to a greater quantity of another kind of pleasure, this is evidence that the former pleasure is superior in kind to the latter. When we look at the evidence, Mill claims, we find that "it is an unquestionable fact that those who are equally acquainted with, and equally capable of appreciating and enjoying, both, do give a most marked preference to the manner of existence which employs their higher faculties."[44] By 'higher faculties' Mill intends the intellect, feelings, imagination, and moral sentiments. Because no competent judge would prefer our contented pig's life to Socrates' life—no matter *how long* the pig might live—Mill famously concludes, "It is better to be a human being dissatisfied than a pig satisfied; better to be Socrates dissatisfied than a fool satisfied."[45] Distinguishing between higher and lower pleasures allows Mill to agree with the critics that the end of human life is not the pursuit of mere animal pleasures while at the same time insisting that the end of life is the pursuit of pleasure nonetheless. It is hardly surprising that the man whose depression was lifted only by reading Wordsworth should deny that the pleasure of push-pin could ever be the equal of the pleasure of poetry. But as this implies, Mill's understanding of human happiness has moved away from Bentham's in important respects.

Mill moves even farther away from Bentham in the course of offering his notorious proof of utilitarianism. Mill sets out to prove that happiness is the ultimate aim towards which all human actions are directed, and, hence, happiness is the ultimate standard by which to judge the rightness or wrongness of actions. Mill concedes, however, that people pursue a variety of goods, including knowledge, virtue, artistic activity, health, and sometimes even money, not merely for the happiness that they bring, but as things worth doing and having for their own sake. That is, he allows that people regard these goods not as mere means to the further end of happiness; rather, they regard these goods as ends-in-themselves. In making this concession Mill is clearly acknowledging the inadequacy of Bentham's account of human motivation and is attempting to connect utilitarianism to a more sophisticated psychology. But in conceding this, doesn't Mill deny his own thesis—for how can he maintain that happiness is the *only thing* desired for its own sake when he allows that we desire a *variety* of goods for their own sake? He argues that there is no contradiction involved, for:

> The ingredients of happiness are very various, and each of them is desirable in itself, and not merely when considered as swelling an aggregate. The principle of utility does not mean that any given pleasure, as music, for instance, or any given exemption from pain, as for example health, are to be looked upon as a means to a collective something termed happiness, and to be desired on that account. They are desired and desirable in and for themselves; besides being means, they are part of the end.[46]

So while Mill allows that humans pursue a variety of goods for their own sake, he argues that these various goods are "ingredients" or "parts" of happiness. But if this is true, happiness cannot simply be an aggregate or collection of unrelated pleasant mental states as Bentham claims. Happiness must be a "concrete whole," as Mill puts it, consisting of a variety of ingredients that one pursues and enjoys over a lifetime.

As Mill moves farther away from Bentham's understanding of happiness, he moves closer to Aristotle's (384-322 B.C.E.). In fact, he attempts to bring together the two distinct conceptions of happiness associated with these philosophers. He consistently expresses his view in hedonistic terms, identifying happiness and pleasure. But his discussion of happiness also reflects *eudaimonism*—the view that happiness consists in the realization of one's distinctively human potentialities. Aristotle famously defended this view in his *Nicomachean Ethics*. Mill follows Aristotle in connecting happiness to the flourishing of one's distinctively human capacities by maintaining that the most valuable forms of pleasure are those that involve the exercise of one's higher faculties. Only those who have cultivated their higher faculties are capable of experiencing the qualitatively superior pleasures associated with their exercise, thereby living more satisfying lives. The doctrine that cultivating one's higher faculties opens up new, superior forms of pleasure implies for Mill, as it did for Aristotle, a crucial distinction between being *content* and being *happy*. Being content simply involves satisfying one's present desires. But with the development of one's higher faculties, one comes to see that some of these desires are not really worthy of being pursued and that pursuing alternative ends would be more satisfying. For example, we may be content as children constantly playing a game like push-pin, but when we mature we come to see that there are more worthy ways to spend our time. The development of our higher faculties, and the consequent refinement of our desires, is at the core of Mill's moral outlook, then. If this is not made plain in *Utilitarianism*, it certainly is in *On Liberty*. Again, Mill insists at the outset that his arguments in this essay are premised on an understanding of utility "in the largest sense, grounded on the permanent interests of man *as a progressive being*" (71, editor's emphasis). What is more, he explicitly endorses the view of the German Hellenist Wilhelm von Humboldt (1767-1835) that "the end of man...is the highest and most harmonious development of his powers to a complete and consistent whole" (112-13).

Though Mill moves in the direction of Aristotle by linking happiness to the realization of what is best in one's nature, there is an important difference in the way that the two understand 'one's nature.' Aristotle thought that the good life is grounded in a *common* human nature, and, hence, his account of happiness is *monistic*. That is to say, he believed that there is *one* lifestyle—the contemplative life of the philosopher—that constitutes true happiness for all human beings. But under the influence of the Romantics, Mill was led to recognize the great diversity within human nature. Individual human beings have unique abilities and inclinations and, hence, there is no one lifestyle that will satisfy all humans. Mill makes this clear in *On Liberty*:

There is no reason that all human existence should be constructed on some one or some small number of patterns. If a person possesses any tolerable amount of common sense and experience, his own mode of laying out his existence is the best, not because it is the best in itself, but because it is his own mode. Human beings are not like sheep; and even sheep are not undistinguishably alike. (122)

Happiness, Mill thinks, involves pursuing a way of life that fulfils the demands of one's own *individual* nature. His account of happiness, then, is *pluralistic*—that is, he allows that there are *many* lifestyles that may be satisfying for humans.

Though our development initially requires the aid and instruction of others, once we have reached maturity—once we 'possess any tolerable amount of common sense and experience,' as Mill puts it—it is essential that we assume control of our own further development. This is because each of us knows what activities and projects will satisfy the demands of our own peculiar nature better than anyone else. Moreover, our capacity to recognize our individual abilities and desires, and our capacity to reflectively choose, or create, a lifestyle that satisfies our individual nature, will develop and flourish only if we exercise those very capacities. Just as one must constantly exercise one's own body in order to maintain and develop one's physical capacities, one must constantly exercise one's mental faculties in order to maintain and develop them. Hence, the realization of one's individuality that is central to human happiness can occur only if it is directed by the individual himself or herself.

We have explored Mill's understanding of happiness in some detail, and this is appropriate given that this is the fundamental concept in his moral philosophy. Now we need to briefly consider what place there is for rules and rights in his utilitarianism. As noted, some critics of utilitarianism argued, even *if* the theory is true, it provides no practical guidance, since "there is not time, previous to action, for calculating and weighing the effects of any line of conduct on the general happiness"[47] Mill allows that it is neither possible nor desirable that we should attempt to calculate the expected utility of every alternative course of action on every single occasion. But, he argues, it is a mistake to think that utilitarianism requires that we attempt such a calculation. Most of the time we properly appeal to moral rules of thumb to guide our behavior. These rules, which enjoin us to keep our promises, tell the truth, and so on, reflect our best knowledge about the likely consequences of various types of actions. Generations worth of human experience has taught us that certain types of actions (promise-keeping and truth-telling, for example) do tend to promote utility, while other types of actions (such as promise-breaking and lying) do not. Our moral rules of thumb reflect the wisdom of the ages, and so rightly guide our behavior on occasions when it is not possible to apply the principle of utility directly. Mill writes,

> It is a strange notion that the acknowledgment of a first principle is inconsistent with the admission of secondary ones....Whatever we adopt as the fundamental principle of morality, we require subordinate principles to apply it by....[48]

The fact that our behavior is guided in large part by these subordinate rules and principles, Mill stresses, does not entail that these rules reflect moral values independent of utility. Rather, our use of these subordinate rules is justified only to the extent that they allow us to effectively and efficiently pursue utility. The principle of utility is so abstract, Mill thought, that it typically cannot be used directly as a decision procedure. Its primary use, Mill says, will be in critically evaluating and resolving conflicts between the secondary rules that do directly guide our behavior.[49]

But other critics argued that even if utilitarianism is workable, it is nevertheless *false*, since it conflicts with some of our most firmly held moral values. "One of the strongest obstacles to the reception of the doctrine that Utility or Happiness is the criterion of right and wrong," Mill writes, "has been drawn from the idea of Justice."[50] Individual rights and principles of justice, the critic contends, place constraints upon the pursuit of utility, and, hence, involve moral values independent of utility. We cannot, for example, enslave a group of people simply because doing so would maximize the greatest good. For the utilitarian to claim that utility is the sole moral value, the critic argues, is tantamount to denying that these constraints exist and to allow that we may sacrifice the welfare of the few when doing so benefits the many. But the fact that we feel so strongly about our rights—as is manifest in our great desire to punish those who infringe them—indicates that these moral values surely do exist. There is, Mill thinks, a sort of fallacy involved in the critic's objection. "Mankind are always predisposed to believe that any subjective feeling, not otherwise accounted for," he writes, "is a revelation of some objective reality."[51] It is a mistake, Mill is suggesting, to conclude that rights exist as moral values independent of utility simply because such powerful feelings are associated with them. In his discussion of the relationship between utility and justice in the final chapter of *Utilitarianism*, Mill aims to demystify rights by providing an account of the strong sentiments surrounding them that is compatible with a utilitarian justification of rights. The interests that rights protect are vital, Mill believes, and, hence, it is quite reasonable that we should feel very strongly about their being safeguarded. Nonetheless, the feelings that are associated with rights have no bearing upon their moral justification.

We have said that Mill's account of happiness is intended to accommodate the variation within human nature. Nevertheless, Mill appreciates that, as members of a single species, all humans share some common interests, and no human can be happy unless these fundamental interests are satisfied. Mill identifies security—by which he means physical safety and security in our possessions—as the most basic of these common interests. Because security involves an "extraordinarily important and impressive kind of utility" and is "the most vital of all interests," it is of the utmost importance for the promotion of the greatest happiness that society protects this most basic human interest.[52] Society does this through a system of rights; and justice, according to Mill, essentially involves the protection of these rights. "Justice," Mill states, "is a name for a certain class of moral rules, which concern the essentials of human well-being more nearly, and are therefore of more absolute obligation, than any other rules for the guidance of life; and the notion which we have found to be of the essence of the idea of justice, that of a right residing in an individual, implies and testifies, to this more binding obligation."[53] We feel that our rights involve very important moral values because of the significant interests they protect. But, again, rights are not fundamental moral values; rather, like all moral considerations, they are reducible to concerns about utility. Society ought to protect our rights, Mill tells us, for "no other reason than general utility."[54] Though principles of justice involve a "more binding obligation" than other moral considerations, they are not perfectly absolute or overriding. Principles of justice often conflict with one another, and in such cases the principle of utility must decide which should govern the case. Moreover, principles of justice may be overruled by considerations of utility when the costs of acting on these principles become intolerably high.

Our discussion of Mill's moral philosophy has identified two fundamental elements of human well-being: security and individuality (the freedom to develop according to one's individual nature). The first element is stressed in *Utilitarianism*, though the second element is suggested by Mill's distinction between higher and lower pleasures. The second element is emphasized in *On Liberty*. As security and individuality are core human interests, they are protected by a right to security and a right to liberty (a right to freely pursue the development of individuality). The fundamental problem is to balance these two general rights and the interests they protect, for it is obvious that in pursuing the development of one's individuality one might infringe upon the security of another. This is the fundamental problem addressed in *On Liberty*.

A SYNOPSIS OF *ON LIBERTY*

Having considered Mill's biography and moral philosophy in some detail, let's turn now to consider *On Liberty* itself. The following summary of the work identifies the primary themes and goals of each of chapter and offers brief explanatory comments on Mill's main arguments.

Chapter I: Introductory

In this opening chapter Mill explains the fundamental issue that he will address, presents a summary of his position on the issue, and explains the general strategy that he will employ to defend his position. The subject of the essay is "the nature and limits of the power which can be legitimately exercised by society over the individual" (63). Mill's fundamental questions is: What rightful limit can be placed on the state's exercise of power through the law and society's exercise of power through public opinion? Mill sees this as a perennial issue in political philosophy, and he opens his essay with a brief sketch of the historical conflict between individual liberty and political authority. The notion of liberty involved here is, to use Isaiah Berlin's term, the notion of "negative freedom,"[55] which identifies liberty with the absence of external coercion over an individual's thought and actions. On this understanding, an individual is free to the extent that she is able to act according to her own inclinations.

   In the past, the primary threat to individual liberty had come from despotic governments that pursued their own interests at the expense of the interests of those governed. Over time, mechanisms developed that allowed subjects to hold rulers accountable. The people claimed to have inviolable rights against the sovereign, and in time they managed to establish institutions to enforce their rights and represent their interests. With the emergence of modern democracies, the people themselves had become sovereign, and some came to believe that a principle of liberty was no longer necessary, since the people did not need to be protected from themselves. But, as de Tocqueville had observed, the rule of the people really amounts to the rule of the majority, and so the possibility of a "tyranny of the majority" becomes a real threat. Moreover, a majority can impose its will upon a minority through informal, nonpolitical sanctions, thereby practicing "a social tyranny more formidable than many kinds of political oppression, since, though not usually upheld by such extreme penalties, it leaves fewer means of escape, penetrating much more deeply into the details of life and enslaving the soul itself" (66). The struggle for individual liberty persists even in the democratic age.

Having articulated and motivated the basic issue to be addressed in the essay, Mill now presents his fundamental position on the issue:

> The object of this essay is to assert one very simple principle, as entitled to govern absolutely the dealings of society with the individual in the way of compulsion and control, whether the means used are physical force in the form of legal penalties or the moral coercion of public opinion. That principle is that the sole end for which mankind are warranted, individually or collectively, in interfering with the liberty of action of any of their number, is self-protection. That the only purpose for which power can be rightfully exercised over any member of a civilized community, against his will, is to prevent harm to others. His own good, either physical or moral, is not a sufficient warrant. He cannot rightfully be compelled to do or forbear because it will be better for him to do so, because it will make him happier, because, in the opinions of others, to do so would be wise, or even right. These are good reasons for remonstrating with him, or reasoning with him, or persuading him, or entreating him, but not for compelling him, or visiting him with any evil in case he does otherwise. To justify that, the conduct from which it is desired to deter him must be calculated to produce evil to someone else. The only part of the conduct of anyone for which he is amenable to society is that which concerns others. In the part which merely concerns himself, his independence is, of right, absolute. Over himself, over his own body and mind, the individual is sovereign. (70-1)

The "one very simple principle" that Mill will defend in the essay—that society may coerce an individual in order to prevent her from acting in a particular way only if acting in that way will cause harm to someone else—is today known as the Harm (or, sometimes, Liberty) Principle. Note that the Harm Principle claims that harm to others is a *necessary* condition for coercion and not a *sufficient* condition. So, while certain conduct might harm others, society still might not be justified in pro-

hibiting it. Note also that while Mill says that there is only *one* principle
involved here, he also emphasizes a second principle that is a logical
corollary of his Harm Principle—namely, that society may not justifiably
coerce an individual if her actions affect no one but herself. This means
that paternalism (coercion for the good of the person being coerced) is
never a sufficient condition for coercion. (Mill himself later refers to "the
principles asserted in these pages" (147, my emphasis).)

Mill immediately qualifies his position, explaining that the Harm
Principle applies "only to human beings in the maturity of their faculties" (71). Children—and presumably the mentally ill, though Mill does
not specify this—may justifiably be coerced for their own good. More
controversially, Mill also claims that the Harm Principle does not apply
to adults in undeveloped societies where free and equal discussion is not
yet possible. He writes,

> we may leave out of consideration those backward states of society
> in which the race itself may be considered as in its nonage....Despo-
> tism is a legitimate mode of government in dealing with barbarians,
> provided the end is their improvement and the means justified by
> actually effecting that end. Liberty, as a principle, has no applica-
> tion to any state of things anterior to the time when mankind have
> become capable of being improved by free and equal discussion.
> (71)

The Harm Principle is an appropriate political principle for a modern
democracy in which free and equal discussion is possible, but it is not
an appropriate principle for societies that have not yet reached that
stage of political maturity. In such societies despotic paternalism—even
when exercised by another society—may be justified, so long as it is
directed towards the social and political development of that society.
Mill's position here is anchored in the view that social development is
historically conditioned. This, as we have seen, is one of the lessons that
he learned from the Coleridgians and St. Simonians. Recall the passage
from his *Autobiography* where he wrote, "all questions of political
institutions are relative, not absolute, and different stages of human
progress not only *will* have, but *ought* to have different institutions."
(Bear in mind too Mill's personal role in administering the affairs of
India.)

Having defined his subject and articulated the fundamental position
that he intends to defend in the essay, Mill next explains how he will
(and will not) go about arguing for his liberty principle:

It is proper to state that I forego any advantage which could be derived to my argument from the idea of abstract right as a thing independent of utility. I regard utility as the ultimate appeal on all ethical questions; but it must be utility in the largest sense, grounded on the permanent interests of man as a progressive being. (71)

Mill regards the principle of utility as the ultimate moral principle, and he aims to show that the Harm Principle is a secondary or subordinate principle whose application is justified because it will in the long run bring about a greater amount of utility (understood "in the largest sense") for all people than any alternative liberty principle.

Mill here rejects an alternative foundation for liberalism, what we might call the "natural rights model." On this model individuals are naturally—that is, prior to the establishment of political institutions—endowed with certain rights, including the rights to acquire and transfer property, the right to self-defense, and the right to punish those who violate one's other natural rights. The model envisages individuals in a pre-political "state of nature" transferring some of these rights to the sovereign through a contractual process. Individuals are motivated to do this because they gain advantages from doing so. The primary function of the sovereign is to protect individual rights, and the individual retains those rights against the state that he does not—or cannot, in the case of inalienable rights—transfer to the sovereign. The rights that the individual retains limit the power of the sovereign and form a private domain over which the individual himself is sovereign. Such is the view of John Locke (1632-1704), Mill's most important predecessor in the English liberal tradition. This model is clearly reflected in the American *Declaration of Independence* (1776) and the French *Declaration of the Rights of Man and Citizen* (1789).

Bentham famously called natural rights "nonsense upon stilts,"[56] and Mill agreed with this assessment. Both Bentham and Mill saw appeals to natural rights as involving a suspect form of moral intuitionism; the content of so-called natural rights merely reflect the moral prejudices and biases of those who assert them. Since he denies that rights are fundamental moral values, Mill thinks that a defense of liberty ultimately cannot be grounded in them. But remember that Mill does believe that it is possible to accommodate rights within a utilitarian framework as *derived moral values*. So when Mill speaks in *On Liberty* of a "right" to freely pursue one's goals so long as one does not infringe the rights of others, we should not immediately conclude that he has abandoned his fundamental utilitarian stance. His rejection of natural rights as basic moral values does not entail a rejection of rights simpliciter.

So in the opening chapter Mill provides us with a preview of the central argument of the essay. A democratic society where the limits of authority over individuals' actions are drawn in accordance with the Harm Principle—that is, a society where liberty of thought and discussion are respected, and individuality is valued and allowed to flourish—will be a happier, more progressive society than one in which individual liberty is more restricted. The Harm Principle insures individual utility, since freedom is a necessary condition for personal development, and social utility, since society as a whole will benefit in a variety of ways from a rich and diverse population.

Chapter II: Of the Liberty of Thought and Discussion

In this chapter Mill presents a classic and highly influential case for the freedom of thought and expression, including the freedom of the press. Mill argues that neither the government acting formally through legislation nor the public acting informally may legitimately suppress the expression of an opinion, even when that opinion is held only by a very small minority. Mill's overarching argument for this conclusion imagines three possible states of affairs. First, it could be the case that the minority opinion is true and the majority opinion is false. If this is the case, and the majority suppresses the minority opinion, society is denied the truth. In suppressing the minority opinion, the majority assumes that its view on the matter is infallible. But, Mill argues, such an assumption is not justified. Human history is replete with examples where the majority has incorrectly assumed that its view was infallibly correct. Mill cites the cases of Socrates and Jesus as two such examples. Second, it is possible that the minority opinion is false and the majority opinion is in fact true. One would think that if the circumstances ever justified suppressing an opinion, this would be it. Mill believes that we are rarely, if ever, in a position to judge that an opinion is infallibly correct. But, even if we grant for the sake of argument the dubious assumption that we are sometimes in a position to know that an opinion is perfectly false, there is, he argues, compelling reason not to suppress the false opinion. If an opinion—even one granted to be infallibly true—is not challenged, it becomes "dead dogma," mere cant, and as such the opinion loses its ability to motivate action. Hence, even false opinions play a vital role in public discourse by allowing us to clearly and vividly understand why a true opinion *is* true. Third, it could be the case that the minority opinion and the majority opinion are both partly true. Mill believes this is typically the case, particularly when it comes to moral and political opinions. He argues that in such cases the truth about the matter emerges through unconstrained discussion of the competing opinions. To stifle either opinion would be to halt this process, and, hence, to prevent the truth about the matter from emerging. In every case then, Mill argues, utility is best promoted—because *truth* is best promoted—by allowing the free expression of the minority opinion. Liberty of thought and discussion is society's most effective means for finding the truth, as elusive as it may be. Hence, a policy of (virtually) absolute liberty of thought and discussion is justified.

There are important assumptions about both the *nature* of knowledge and truth and the *process* by which we acquire knowledge and truth underlying Mill's arguments here, which he identifies in the following passage:

> The beliefs which we have most warrant for have no safeguard to rest on, but a standing invitation to the whole world to prove them unfounded. If the challenge is not accepted, or is accepted and the attempt fails, we are far enough from certainty still, but we have done the best that the existing state of human reason admits of— we have neglected nothing that could give the truth a chance of reaching us; if the lists are kept open, we may hope that if there is a better truth, it will be found when the human mind is capable of receiving it; and in the meantime we may rely on having attained such approach to truth as is possible in our own day. This is the amount of certainty attainable by a fallible being, and this the sole way of attaining it. (81)

Mill here endorses a form of fallibilism (the doctrine that even our most well justified opinions are fallible and open to revision in light of future evidence). On this view, an opinion is justified to the extent that the evidence supporting that opinion is, on balance, stronger than the countervailing evidence. As new evidence on the matter emerges, we must consider whether that evidence supports the received opinion or whether it better supports some competing view. Mill regards the offering and assessing of evidence as a collective pursuit—this is the general purpose of public discourse—and he takes the political implications of this epistemic position to be clear. "Complete liberty of contradicting and disproving our opinion is the very condition which justifies us in assuming its truth for purposes of action;" he writes, "and on no other terms can a being with human faculties have any rational assurance of being right" (79-80). To bar the expression of an opinion that is contrary to received opinion is to willfully ignore evidence that is relevant to the matter, and, hence, is to impede the pursuit of knowledge. Fallibilism, Mill contends, entails robust liberty of thought and discussion. This is particularly so given that over the course of human history received opinion has been mistaken more often than not.

But Mill is thinking here not only about what it is for an opinion to be *justified*, but also what it is for an opinion to be *genuinely our own*. People who "have never thrown themselves into the mental position of those who think differently from them and considered what such persons may have to say...do not, in any proper sense of the word, know the doctrine which they themselves profess" (95). Here again Mill's own biography provides a helpful example. As a young man Mill came to believe that Bentham's disciples had completely closed themselves off from considering contrary positions that might have some grain of truth to them. Like one of the battling knights in the medieval allegory, they did not even consider that the shield may be a different color on the opposite side. Because they were unwilling to consider their opponents' opinions in a meaningful way and to revise their own beliefs in light of the insights of others, they did not really understand the doctrine they themselves advocated. They were merely parroting the views of Bentham. The young Mill, on the other hand, actively sought to engage his opponents and to genuinely understand their positions. Like the third knight of the allegory, he believed that to know the truth one must look at both sides of the shield. He then revised his own views in light of what he found to be reasonable in his opponents' views. As a result of this process, he believed that his own views were not only better justified and more nearly true, but they were truly his own.

Mill does recognize certain limits to the freedom of expression. Again, the mere fact that an opinion conflicts with popular opinion, or is regarded as offensive by some, is never sufficient reason to suppress that opinion through either formal or informal coercion. But, he writes at the opening of the third chapter, "even opinions lose their immunity when the circumstances in which they are expressed are such as to constitute their expression a positive instigation to some mischievous act" (111). Here Mill anticipates the famous Clear and Present Danger Test for determining whether speech is protected by the First Amendment that was articulated by Justice Oliver Wendell Holmes (1841-1932). In *Schenck v. United States*, Holmes wrote, "The question in every case is whether the words used are in such circumstances and are of such a nature as to create a clear and present danger that they will bring about the substantive evils that Congress has a right to prevent."[57] Mill contrasts the case of someone who expresses the opinion that corn dealers are starving the poor in a newspaper article with the case of someone who shouts the same opinion to an angry mob that has gathered in front of a corn dealer's house. The expression of the opinion in the latter case may legitimately be suppressed, since in this context it is very likely to lead to harm and thereby violate the Harm Principle, but the expression of the opinion in the former case may not be likewise suppressed. Mill's point here is also related to his understanding of the nature and aim of public discourse. For Mill, the fundamental goal of public discourse is to find truth by offering and assessing the evidence related to competing opinions. Publishing an article in a newspaper contributes in a productive manner to the goal of public discourse, but inciting a mob to riot does not.

Chapter III: Of Individuality, as One of the Elements of Well-Being

In the second chapter Mill argued that we should be free to *form* and *express* opinions, and now in the third chapter he argues that we should be free to *act* on these opinions, so long as doing so does not harm others. He aims to show that, just as it is useful that different opinions should be expressed, it is useful that "there should be different experiments of living; that free scope should be given to varieties of character, short of injury to others..." (112) So, in matters that concern only ourselves, we should be free to live our lives as we see fit, pursuing the ends we choose and shaping our own character. "Where not the person's own character but the traditions or customs of other people are the rule of conduct," Mill argues, "there is wanting one of the principal ingredients of human happiness, and quite the chief ingredient of individual and social progress" (112) For Mill, individuality is valuable both as an expression of what is best in human life and as a means for individual and social improvement.

Mill essentially asks us to consider two societies: one in which human actions are determined by tradition and custom, and another in which human actions arise freely from the character of individual human beings. In which society is human happiness maximized? We must, of course, be clear about what Mill means by 'happiness.' As noted in our discussion of his utilitarianism, Mill's official position is hedonism—happiness is identified with pleasurable experiences. But, again, Mill's distinction between qualitatively higher and lower pleasures suggests a move away from hedonism towards the Aristotelian ideal of self-development, for the enjoyment of higher pleasures requires the cultivation and exercise of our distinctively human faculties. The influence of the German Hellenist Wilhelm von Humboldt on Mill's understanding of human happiness is evident throughout this chapter. (Indeed, the epigraph of *On Liberty* is a quote from von Humboldt's *The Sphere and Duties of Government*.) Mill approvingly cites von Humboldt's claim that "the end of man...is the highest and most harmonious development of his powers to a complete and consistent whole" (112-3) The question then is, in which of our two societies will the greatest number of individuals be able to develop their distinctively human powers to a complete and consistent whole?

Consider first an individual who is required by formal or informal sanctions to act as custom dictates. Mill writes of this individual,

> though the customs are both good as customs and suitable to him, yet to conform to custom merely *as* custom does not educate or develop in him any of the qualities which are the distinctive endowment of a human being. The human faculties of perception, judgment, discriminative feeling, mental activity, and even moral preference are exercised only in making a choice. He who does anything because it is the custom makes no choice. He gains no practice either in discerning or in desiring what is best. The mental and moral, like the muscular powers, are improved only by being used. The faculties are called into no exercise by doing a thing merely because others do it, no more than by believing a thing only because others believe it. If the grounds of an opinion are not conclusive to the person's own reason, his reason cannot be strengthened, but is likely to be weakened by his adopting it: and if the inducements to an act are not such as are consentaneous to his own feelings and character (where affection, or the rights of others, are not concerned), it is so much done towards rendering his feelings and character inert and torpid instead of active and energetic. (113-4)

Living one's life merely according to the customs of one's society involves a number of deficiencies. First, the customs of society may not fit an individual's character. "Human nature is not a machine to be built after a model"

(114), Mill explains; hence, the customs of a society will not be suited to all of its members. But even where a culture's traditions *do happen to fit* an individual's nature, if one adopts these customs merely because they are customs, then one's character is not truly one's own. Mill's argument here directly parallels his argument in chapter two—that if one does not critically evaluate one's views in light of alternative views, then they are not really one's *own* views at all. With respect to character, Mill writes, "One whose desires and impulses are not his own has no character, no more than a steam-engine has a character" (115). But most importantly, one who merely adopts customary ways of life "has no need of any other faculty than the ape-like one of imitation" (114). If people do not take an active role in determining how to live their lives, they will not cultivate their higher faculties, the exercise of which constitutes happiness.

Mill offers empirical evidence to support his claims here. He points to the China of his day as the paradigm of a stagnant society that has suffered the stultifying effects of its citizenry living according to custom and tradition. But he thought that one hardly needed to look to the other side of the world to see the ill-effects of conformity. Even in Europe, and England in particular, "individual spontaneity is hardly recognized by the common modes of thinking as having any intrinsic worth or deserving any regard on its own account" (112). Mill largely attributes this sorry state of affairs to a Protestant doctrine of self-abnegation articulated by the likes of the French Reformer John Calvin (1509-64), a frequent target of attack for Mill. Victorian morality, Mill suggests, is simply the latest incarnation of this general doctrine of self-denial and submission. "In our times," he writes, "from the highest class of society down to the lowest, everyone lives as under the eye of a hostile and dreaded censorship" (116). Mill himself surely felt just such censorship in his relationship with Harriet Taylor. Mill says that when he observes his contemporaries making important decisions about how to conduct their lives, they do not ask themselves, what do *I* prefer, or what would suit *my own* inclinations and bring out the best in *me*? Rather, they ask themselves, what do *others* expect me to prefer, or, worse yet, what would *others in a higher social class* prefer? Mill argues that when people think in this way, it is not simply that they ignore their own individual nature, rather, it is an indication that they utterly lack any individual character. They simply take their life-plans from others, letting public opinion determine what is worth knowing and doing. Mill claims that the homogenizing effects of public opinion on the character of the English populace are clearly evident. "Comparatively speaking," he writes, "they now read the same things, listen to the same things, see the same things, go to the same places, have their hopes and fears directed to the same objects..." (127). The force of public opinion is, he asserts, fast leading to deadening uniformity and conformity.

Consider now an individual living in a society where he is left free to plan his own life and to form his own character.

> He who chooses his plan for himself, employs all his faculties. He must use observation to see, reasoning and judgment to foresee, activity to gather materials for decision, discrimination to decide, and when he has decided, firmness and self-control to hold to his deliberate decision. And these qualities he requires and exercises exactly in proportion as the part of his conduct which he determines according to his own judgment and feelings is a large one. (114)

Individuality—freely pursuing a way of life that satisfy the demands of one's peculiar nature—requires the development of all of one's faculty *and at the same time* is the expression of what is best in human life. But individuality is essential not only to *individual* well-being, it is also a vital to *social* progress and, hence, to promoting the general good. Mill writes, "In proportion to the development of his individuality, each person becomes more valuable to himself, and is therefore capable of being more valuable to others" (118). Persons endowed with originality and genius, who engage in experiments in living, are invaluable to society because they introduce a wide (and often superior) range of alternative lifestyles from which everyone may choose.

Mill takes the political implications of the comparison of these two societies to be obvious: "the only unfailing and permanent source of [individual and social] improvement is liberty" (125). Individual freedom is the principal condition for individuality, and individuality is one of the fundamental elements of human well-being. Hence, we should give individual freedom the widest latitude possible. That is, we should recognize a sphere of non-interference that extends to the point where an individual's free actions interfere with the freedom of others. This is precisely what the Harm Principle does, and here then is the core of Mill's utilitarian defense of this principle.

Chapter IV: Of the Limits to the Authority of Society over the Individual

Chapter four examines how the Harm Principle may be reasonably interpreted and applied. It opens with Mill reaffirming his general position that social coercion is justified only in those cases where an individual's conduct harms the interests of others and not in those cases where an individual's conduct harms only his or her own interests. He bolsters his earlier arguments against paternalism, arguing that, since each individual knows his own interests and inclinations better than anyone else and the individual is more motivated to tend to his well-being than others, the individual, and not others, must be the final judge of what is good for him. Having established in the previous chapter that individual autonomy is a basic good, Mill concludes here that, "All errors which [an individual] is likely to commit against advice and warning are far outweighed by the evil of allowing others to constrain him to what they deem his good" (131).

Mill is quick to point out that his anti-paternalistic stance should not be understood as selfish indifference. Humans must take an active interest in other individuals' self-development:

> Human beings owe to each other help to distinguish the better from the worse, and encouragement to choose the former and avoid the latter. They should be forever stimulating each other to increased exercise of their higher faculties and increased direction of their feelings and aims towards wise instead of foolish, elevating instead of degrading, objects and contemplations. (130)

Mill allows that we may attempt to *persuade* individuals that they are acting contrary to their own good—indeed, he claims that we do not do this nearly enough—but we may not apply either formal or informal sanctions when a person's conduct harms no one besides himself. Mill explores the vague boundary between persuasion and coercion in some detail.

Mill recognizes that his Harm Principle entails a fundamental distinction between "self-regarding" and "other-regarding" actions. He has argued that we must respect individual autonomy in cases where no one else's interests are affected, but we may legitimately coerce people when others are harmed by their conduct. But Mill himself recognizes that this distinction is open to challenge:

> The distinction here pointed out between the part of a person's life which concerns only himself and that which concerns others, many persons will refuse to admit. How (it may be asked) can any part of the conduct of a member of society be a matter of indifference to the other members? No person is an entirely isolated being; it is

impossible for a person to do anything seriously or permanently hurtful to himself without mischief reaching at least to his near connections, and often far beyond them. (133–34)

How then does Mill think this distinction can be maintained? He writes that when "a person is led to violate a distinct and assignable obligation to any other person or persons, the case is taken out of the self-regarding class and becomes amenable to moral disapprobation in the proper sense of the term" (135). To illustrate this claim Mill offers the case of an intemperate man who is unable to pay his debts and fulfill his responsibilities to his family because of his behavior. The man is culpable for neglecting his duties to his creditors and family, but not for the intemperate behavior itself. Similarly, if he were a soldier or policeman who was unable to fulfill his public duty because of his intemperate behavior, he would be guilty of a social offense. The implication is that if the man were able to fulfill his specific duties to his creditors, family, and the public, the Harm Principle would provide no reason to interfere with his behavior. As Mill puts it, if the conduct "neither violates any specific duty to the public nor occasions perceptible hurt to any assignable individual except himself, the inconvenience is one which society can afford to bear, for the sake of the greater good of human freedom" (135-6).

In the second-half of chapter four Mill applies the Harm Principle to a series of extended, real-life examples. In addition to clarifying the meaning of the principle, he intends "to show that the principle I maintain is of serious and practical moment, and that I am not endeavoring to erect a barrier against imaginary evils" (138). Among the cases that Mill considers are: Muslim societies that prohibit the eating of pork, Catholic societies that impose celibacy upon non-Catholic clergy, the temperance movement in the United States and England, Sabbatarian legislation (so-called "blue laws" that restrict conduct on the Sabbath), and the suppression of Mormonism in America. In all of these cases there are two main motivations for repressing the conduct involved. First, there are paternalistic motivations—those seeking to prohibit the conduct genuinely believe that to engage in the conduct is bad for the person who would do so. Second, those seeking to prohibit the conduct "have a distaste for [the conduct], and resent it as an outrage to their feelings" (137). Mill argues that in all of these cases there is an encroachment upon "the most unquestionably legitimate liberty of the individual" (138). The Harm Principle does not sanction coercion in any of these cases, Mill contends, because the conduct involved is self-regarding, and mere offense to the moral sensibilities others does not really constitute harm to others.

Chapter V: Applications

In this final chapter Mill addresses more interpretive issues raised by the Harm Principle. He begins by making it clear that the Harm Principle expresses a *necessary* but not a *sufficient* condition for social coercion. It is not Mill's view that we may justifiably prevent others from acting whenever they will harm others. He writes,

> it must by no means be supposed, because damage, or probability of damage, to the interests of others can alone justify the interference of society, that therefore it always does justify such interference. In many cases, an individual, in pursuing a legitimate object, necessarily and therefore legitimately causes pain or loss to others, or intercepts a good which they had a reasonable hope of obtaining. (147-8)

Mill asks us to consider the case of a competitive examination or an athletic event. While he is willing to say that one individual (the "winner") has harmed another's (the "loser's") interests, he does not think that we should do away with competitive exams and athletic events; for "it is, by common admission, better for the general interest of mankind that persons should pursue their object undeterred by this sort of consequence" (148) The Harm Principle then is a "triggering" principle: when we recognize that some form of behavior harms others, we must closely scrutinize it and consider whether the benefits of allowing people to engage in that behavior outweigh the harms caused by the behavior. In the previous chapter Mill put the point this way, "As soon as any part of a person's conduct affects prejudicially the interests of others, society has jurisdiction over it, and the question whether the general welfare will or will not be promoted by interfering with it becomes open to discussion" (130)

Mill discusses the extent to which individual liberty may be justifiably restricted in order to prevent crimes and accidents. Preventing crimes and accidents is a legitimate function of government, and Mill allows that individual freedom may be limited to some extent in order to further these social goals. He offers examples of measures that the state may legitimately adopt in its preventative function. He suggests a number of regulations related to the sale of goods, such as poisons, that might be used for harmful purposes (one might consider the implications of Mill's discussion here for the sale of handguns), and he argues that the conduct of individuals with a history of harmful behavior may be restricted in certain ways (one might consider the implications for preventing drunk driving here).

A related topic involves whether the state may take measures that have the effect of discouraging certain forms of behavior, while refraining from prohibiting the behavior outright. For example, may the state impose so-called "sin taxes" on certain goods such as alcohol or cigarettes? Mill explains that we must be very clear about the justifying purposes of these measures. Taxation for fiscal purposes is legitimate, and the state may tax goods for this purpose, though doing so may mean that some people will not be able to afford to buy certain goods. But to tax goods at a rate beyond what is required for fiscal purposes in order to discourage some sort of self-regarding conduct is illegitimate.

Mill next raises the very interesting question of whether individuals should be free to sell themselves into slavery. We can certainly imagine circumstances where doing so would be a purely self-regarding act, seeming to fall outside the scope of the Harm Principle. But Mill argues that our right to liberty does not permit us to enter into such a contract. By selling oneself into slavery, Mill argues, one relinquishes one's future liberty, and thereby "defeats, in his own case, the very purpose which is the justification of allowing him to dispose of himself" (155). It is inconsistent, Mill maintains, to appeal to one's freedom in order to justify voluntarily relinquishing one's freedom. Many commentators have been puzzled by Mill's argument here (as we will see in the following section), since it seems to be a departure from both his general position and his utilitarian mode of argument. Indeed, Mill's argument, which points out the self-defeating nature of voluntarily enslaving oneself, looks very much like the sort of argument that the utilitarians' nonconsequentialist rival Immanuel Kant would offer.

Given Mill's central concern about unjust encroachments upon individual liberty, it is perhaps surprising to find him arguing that in certain cases the state does not interfere with the individual *enough*. This is particularly so in the case of familial relations; "a case," Mill says, "in its direct influence on human happiness, more important than all others taken together" (157). The state must eliminate the despotic powers that marriage confers upon a husband by extending and protecting the rights of women. With respect to children, Mill argues that the state should do much more by way of forcing parents to educate their children. Nonetheless, he expresses strong reservations about public education, both because parents may legitimately disagree about the content of their children's education and because public education is too likely to encourage the sort of mass conformity that he so deplores. Mill even goes so far as to endorse laws that forbid marriage unless the parties can show they have the means of supporting a family. His reasoning is straightforwardly utilitarian: "to bring a child into existence without a fair prospect of being able, not only to provide food for its body, but instruction and training for its mind, is a moral crime, both against the unfortunate offspring and against society" (158)

Having offered numerous arguments for the conclusion that the state should not interfere with individual liberty except in those cases where others are harmed, Mill, in his final discussion of the essay, makes the case that government should not interfere with the conduct of citizens in general, *even when that interference would not encroach upon their liberty and is intended to help them.* Mill presents three objections to government interference in general. First, the government should refrain from interfering "when the thing being done is likely to be better done by individuals than by the government" (161). This reflects the basic rationale for a free-market economy. Second, even in cases where the government might do the thing better than private individuals, the government should refrain if the thing is a means to the "mental education" of the citizenry. Examples of these sorts of things include: citizens participating in trials as jurors, citizens taking leading roles in local government, and citizens directing philanthropic enterprises. Tocqueville's influence here is clear. These are all activities that foster the sort of civic education that is necessary to unite and vitalize a democracy. The third reason for limiting government interference in general is that it prevents "the great evil of adding unnecessarily to [the government's] power" (162).

INTERPRETIVE AND CRITICAL ISSUES

Now that we have a sketch of the main themes and arguments of *On Liberty* before us, we can consider some of the main interpretive and critical issues raised by the work. Even Mill's most sympathetic readers acknowledge that his claim that this essay articulates a "very simple" principle is misleading. The Harm Principle is an abstract, general principle, and, despite Mill's attempts to elucidate the meaning and implications of the principle, many of its core concepts and ramifications remain unclear. Moreover, critics have challenged Mill's arguments in support of the Harm Principle ever since the initial publication of the essay.[58] Thomas Carlyle, one of the figures that Mill credits for having expanded his narrow creed of Benthamite utilitarianism, reacted in his usual trenchant manner, writing in a letter to his brother, "As if it were a sin to control or coerce into better methods human swine in any way...Ach Gott in Himmel [Alas, God in heaven]!"[59] The most comprehensive of Mill's early critics was the British legal historian and judge James Fitz-james Stephen (1828-94), whose *Liberty, Equality, Fraternity* (1873) provides a line-by-line critique of *On Liberty*. Some more recent commentators have raised new problems for Mill's view, while others have attempted to defend and develop his view. This section identifies a number of the fundamental and perennial issues raised by *On Liberty*. The aim here is not to defend any particular view on these issues, but to indicate important questions for the reader to consider in analyzing and evaluating Mill's view.

Questions about the Meaning and Application of the Harm Principle

Is the distinction between self-regarding and other-regarding actions tenable?

As we have seen, Mill's Harm Principle suggests a distinction between two types of actions: those, on the one hand, that affect only the agent himself or herself, and those, on the other hand, that may potentially affect other people. The Harm Principle prohibits the use of legal and social coercion to repress the first type of action. But many critics have questioned the existence of purely "self-regarding" actions, since almost anything that an individual does affects others in some way. Stephen, for example, writes:

> I think that the attempt to distinguish between self-regarding acts and acts which regard others, is like an attempt to distinguish between acts which happen in time and acts which happen in space. Every act happens at some time and in some place, and in like manner every act that we do either does or may affect both ourselves and others. I think therefore, that the distinction (which, by the way, is not at all a common one) is altogether fallacious and unfounded.... [The Harm Principle] assumes that some acts regard

the agent only, and that some regard other people. In fact, by far the most important part of our conduct regards both ourselves and others.[60]

The implication of Stephen's denial that there are purely self-regarding actions is straightforward: if there is no sphere of self-regarding action, then the Harm Principle is vacuous and the realm of individual liberty is nil.

In an influential analysis, J.C. Rees defends Mill against this objection by arguing that his view rests upon a crucial distinction between an act's "affecting others" and an act's "affecting *the interests* of others."[61] Mill's principle is not intended to demarcate an area of conduct that has no effects whatsoever upon other people, Rees argues. Mill himself concedes in Chapter IV that all of our actions may affect others in *some* manner. The point, rather, is that only *certain* effects of our actions upon others should be taken into account in determining whether or not to prohibit conduct. The only relevant effects of our actions are those that negatively affect the interests of others. An action can affect others without damaging their interests, and this is the sort of action that may not legitimately be prohibited. But what precisely are "interests"?

What exactly constitutes 'harm'?

Quite obviously, unless we know exactly what Mill means by 'harm,' the Harm Principle will be empty and useless. Rees's response to the preceding question implies that harm involves a setback to one's interests. This understanding of harm is developed at length by Joel Feinberg in *Harm to Others* (1984). Critics of this approach to analyzing harm point out that the question about the nature and content of our interests—and, hence, the question about what constitutes harm—is highly controversial and cannot be answered without an appeal to contestable moral beliefs. While it may be clear that physical injuries and injuries to property should count as harms for purposes of the Harm Principle, it is wholly unclear whether other sorts of injuries should be construed as harms.

The problem here can be illustrated by considering the Harm Principle in its application to several cases. Recall that Mill applies the Harm Principle to a number of cases in the second-half of Chapter IV in order to better elucidate its meaning. In one case he argues that the Harm Principle does not authorize the prohibition of the eating of pork in Islamic countries, despite the fact that Muslims regard the act as deeply offensive. Why, precisely, does avoiding such psychological harm not amount to an interest, or, if it is acknowledged to be an interest, why is it not an interest worthy of protection? Clearly the offended Muslims think that they have an interest in avoiding such offense. For his part, Mill cannot simply claim that it is self-evident that avoiding such offense is not an interest to be protected, since this smacks of the moral intuitionism that he scorned. Consider now the contemporary debates about whether the Harm Principle sanctions the censorship of pornography and hate speech.[62] Some contend that pornography and hate speech *indirectly* harm women and minorities by promoting a social environment that makes violence against women and minorities more likely. Such violence is regarded as an uncontroversial instance of harm, and the debate here typically relates to empirical questions about whether or not pornography and hate speech really have these effects. But others contend that pornography and hate speech *directly* harm women and minorities by degrading them. Does this sort of degradation amount to a form of psychological or emotional harm? Some people think that it clearly does, but others do not. Since Mill does not provide us with a clear, non-controversial account of our interests (supposing that such an account is even possible), his understanding of the nature of harm remains elusive.

To what extent, if any, should the Harm Principle encompass harm to society?

The issue here is whether the Harm Principle should limit its consideration to harm done to other discrete individuals, or should take into account broader harms to society, including both its political institutions and social institutions (such as the family). This issue was central to a famous exchange between the English judge Lord Patrick Devlin (1905-92) and H.L.A. Hart (1907-92), arguably the most important legal philosopher of the 20th century. The Hart-Devlin debate developed in response to the *Report of the Departmental Committee on Homosexual Offences and Prostitution* (The Wolfenden Report) issued in 1957. The Wolfenden Committee was charged with reviewing English law governing prostitution and homosexuality. The Committee's report argued, very much in the spirit of Mill, that "there must remain a realm of private morality and immorality which is, in brief and crude terms, not the law's business." The *Report* recommended that homosexual behavior between consenting adults in private should no longer be a crime.

Devlin rejected the *Report's* fundamental premise, arguing there is no sphere of private morality that is in principle beyond the scope of the law.[63] Devlin claimed that society depends for its survival upon the existence of a shared and binding moral code. (It was not Devlin's aim to defend any particular conception of morality; rather, his point was that social cohesion depends of necessity on the presence of *some* common morality.) To the extent that conduct which is immoral (relative to the social morality involved) threatens the common morality, it is harmful to society itself. For this reason, society has a right to protect itself from disintegration through the legal enforcement of its moral norms. Contrary to the Wolfenden Committee, no conduct is in principle "not the law's business." If consensual homosexual behavior has the effect of eroding social institutions, such as marriage and the family, or undermining fundamental social values, it may rightly be prohibited by the law.

Hart responded in *Law, Liberty, and Morality* (1963) to Devlin's arguments. He defended a revised version of Mill's principle, which involved his well-known distinction between the "positive morality" and the "critical morality" of a society. The former consists of the conventional moral opinions of a community, while the latter consists of the rational moral principles that are employed to assess social institutions and norms, including the norms of positive morality. For example, principles of critical morality may be employed to criticize a society that regards homosexuality as immoral. Following Mill's lead, Hart rejected the use of law to enforce positive morality. He defended the liberal view that society does not depend upon uniformity of moral belief, and argued that, even if social cohesion did require some common moral principles, it is not at all clear that a precept against homosexuality was necessarily among them. At any rate, Hart argued, the burden of proof falls upon those who would prohibit conduct, and, since Lord Devlin's case was utterly lacking empirical support, it is unacceptable.

The Hart-Devlin debate revived interest in Mill's political philosophy. Many of the best known Anglo-American political and legal philosophers considered the implications of Mill's ideas for modern liberal society. Some critics were deeply troubled by these implications. Conservatives, on the one hand, and more radical critics, on the other, saw in Mill an excessive commitment to individualism. Liberal theorists, inspired by Mill's thought (even when they departed from it in important ways), defended the basic principle that individuals should be afforded a substantial realm of personal liberty—including liberty of conscience, speech, and, as Hart's argument shows, sexuality—that the state should not interfere with except to protect others from harm.

Questions about Mill's Utilitarian Strategy

Is Mill's defense of individual liberty really a utilitarian one?

This question might seem surprising given Mill's explicit statement in Chapter I that he 'regards utility as the ultimate appeal on all ethical questions' (71). Nonetheless, many commentators have argued that non-utilitarian considerations are really at the core of the work. Gertrude Himmelfarb, for example, writes:

> Whatever Mill's intentions elsewhere—in his book on *Utilitarianism*, for example—it was not his intention here, in *On Liberty*, to rest his case on utilitarian principles. He occasionally, very occasionally, used the word 'utility', more often 'interests'; but he also used such non-utilitarian words as 'rights' and 'development'. In any event, his primary concern was to establish liberty, not utility, as the sole principle governing the relations of the individual in society.[64]

Himmelfarb's contention that Mill did not even *intend* to defend liberty on the grounds of its utility is rejected by most commentators. Certainly the fact that Mill employs concepts such as 'rights' and 'development,' which are typically associated with deontological or eudaimonistic ethics as opposed to a utilitarian ethic, is not evidence for Himmelfarb's claim. As our discussion of Mill's utilitarianism indicated, he intended to account for these moral values within the context of his expanded utilitarian framework. Recall his claim that utility is best promoted by recognizing rights and principles of justice that constrain the unfettered pursuit of utility, since these rights and principles protect basic interests. Recall, too, that self-development is fundamental to Mill's conception of human happiness.

James Fitzjames Stephen accused Mill of abandoning utilitarianism precisely because he rejected Mill's revisions of Bentham's doctrine. In his three-volume history *The English Utilitarians* (1900), Fitzjames Stephen's brother, Leslie Stephen (1832-1904), writes:

> The most elaborate attack upon the *Liberty* is contained in *Liberty, Equality, Fraternity* (1873), by my brother....The most remarkable point is that the book is substantially a criticism of Mill's [scheme] from the older Utilitarian point of view. It shows, therefore, how Mill diverged from Bentham.[65]

Specifically, Stephen rejected Mill's indirect approach to promoting utility by recognizing general precepts that constrain the direct pursuit of utility. Stephen says:

> There are some acts, opinions, thoughts, and feelings which for various reasons people call good, and others which for other reasons they call bad. They usually wish to promote and encourage the one and to prevent the other. In order to do this they must use promises and threats. I say that the expediency of doing this in any particular case must depend on the circumstances of the case, upon the nature of the act prevented, and the nature of the means by which it can be prevented; and that the attempt to lay down general principles like Mr. Mill's fails....[66]

If restricting someone's liberty in a particular case will certainly increase utility, Stephen is saying, then, surely, a strict utilitarian should favor restricting that person's liberty. Mill's resolute devotion to the Harm Principle in the face of such cases suggests to Stephen—as it has to many subsequent readers—that Mill is advocating an absolute right to personal freedom, which is inconsistent with utilitarianism.

Questions about Mill's Empirical Assumptions

Does extensive personal freedom really promote human happiness?

Some readers of *On Liberty* worry that Mill fails to provide sufficient evidence to support his most fundamental empirical claim—namely, that extensive personal liberty promotes happiness. One of the leading liberal thinkers of the 20th century, Isaiah Berlin (1909-97), expresses this concern:

> It might be argued that there is no *a priori* reason for supposing that most men would not be happier—if that is the goal—in a wholly socialized world where private life and personal freedom are reduced to a vanishing point, than in Mill's individualist order; and that whether this is so or not is a matter for experimental verification.[67]

Of course, Berlin is not here endorsing the view that humans would in fact be happier under a totalitarian regime; his point is merely that it is possible that Mill's assumption about the relation between freedom and happiness is simply wrong, and Mill must provide more empirical evidence to support his claim. After all, Mill's own empiricism demands this of him. The fact that Mill does not bother to produce more evidence suggests to Berlin that establishing the link between freedom and happiness is not at the heart of Mill's view. Berlin maintains that "At the centre of

Mill's thought and feeling lies, not his utilitarianism,...but his passionate belief that men are made human by their capacity for choice—choice of evil and good equally."[68]

Stephen goes further than Berlin, arguing that human nature *does* in fact better develop under conditions of repression than freedom:

> The great defect of Mr. Mill's later writings seems to me to be that he has formed too favourable an estimate of human nature. This displays itself in [Chapter III: Of Individuality, As One of the Elements of Well-Being] by the tacit assumption which pervades every part of it that the removal of restraints usually tends to invigorate character. Surely the very opposite of this is the truth. Habitual exertion is the greatest of all invigorators of character, and restraint and coercion in one form or another is the great stimulus to exertion. If you wish to destroy originality and vigour of character, no way to do so is so sure as to put a high level of comfort easily within the reach of moderate and commonplace exertion. A life made up of danger, vicissitude, and exposure is the sort of life which produces originality and resource.[69]

Stephen's own argument is utterly lacking empirical evidence, but it does suggest a plausible view contrary to Mill's. So, the need for further evidence on both sides is imperative.

Do individuals really know best what is in their own self interest and, if so, do they inevitably pursue it?

Stephen identifies, and challenges, one of the key premises in Mill's argument against paternalism when he writes:

> [Mill supposes that] in all the countries which we are accustomed to call civilized the mass of adults are so well acquainted with their own interests and so much disposed to pursue them that no compulsion or restraint put upon any of them by any others for the purpose of promoting their interests can really promote them. No one can doubt the importance of this assertion, but where is the proof of it?[70]

Human imperfection is a recurring theme in conservative political philosophy, so it is not surprising that Stephen should reject Mill's premise. Even the average adult, Stephen suggests, tends not to know what is truly in her own best interests, and, even if she does, she often does not pursue it due to weakness of will. But if the average adult is cognitively and morally imperfect in these ways, then it seems foolish to insist that utility will be maximized by leaving them to their own devices. Utility would be better maximized by the sort of benevolent despotism that Mill allows for in the case of immature individuals and societies.

Even some of Mill's most sympathetic commentators are deeply skeptical about Mill's assumption here. For example, Hart writes in *Law, Liberty and Morality*:

> No doubt if we no longer sympathise with [Mill's argument against paternalism] this is due, in part, to a general decline in the belief that individuals know their own interests best, and to an increased awareness of a great range of factors which diminish the significance to be attached to an apparently free choice or to consent. Choices may be made or consent given without adequate reflection or appreciation of the consequences; or in pursuit of merely transitory desires; or in various predicaments when the judgment is likely to be clouded; or under inner psychological compulsion; or under pressure by others of a kind too subtle to be susceptible of proof in a law court. Underlying Mill's extreme fear of paternalism there is perhaps a conception of what a normal human being is like which now seems not to correspond to the facts. Mill, in fact, endows him with too much of the psychology of a middle-aged man whose desires are relatively fixed, not liable to be artificially stimulated by external influences; who knows what he wants and what gives him satisfaction or happiness; and who pursues these things when he can.[71]

These considerations led Hart to conclude that, in addition to preventing harm to others, the law may be legitimately used for some restricted forms of paternalism, restraining people from engaging in behavior that is severely harmful only to themselves.

A Question about Mill's Argument against Paternalism

Would rational individuals willingly consent to certain forms of paternalism?

In his classic analysis of Mill's argument against paternalism, Gerald Dworkin is led to the same conclusion as Hart, though by a different route. Dworkin suggests that "since we are all aware of our irrational propensities, deficiencies in cognitive and emotional capacities, and unavoidable and avoidable ignorance, it is rational and prudent for us to in effect take out 'social insurance policies.'"[72] These social insurance policies take the form of paternalistic laws that either require or prohibit certain forms of behavior that Mill would call "self-regarding." Dworkin identifies three general (and often overlapping) types of situations in which it seems plausible that fully rational people would agree to have paternalistic restrictions imposed upon them. The first involves attaining fundamental or basic goods, such as health and education, which are necessary for pursuing the good life—whatever one's conception of the good life might be. The second class of cases involve behavior that has irreversible, far-reaching, and dangerous consequences; for example, taking addictive drugs that destroy one's mental and physical capacities. The third type of situation is where the individual involved does not understand or correctly appreciate the dangers related to the behavior. One might not, for example, know the true extent of the risks associated with cigarette smoking. Dworkin concludes, in short, that "we would be most likely to consent to paternalism in those instances in which it preserves and enhances for the individual his ability to rationally consider and carry out his own decisions."[73]

Dworkin's argument for limited paternalism is clearly not utilitarian, for it is premised upon the absolute value of free choice and a certain conception of what it means to be a person. On this view, coercing someone—even for his own good—is wrong because it denies the individual's status as an autonomous agent. Nonetheless, Dworkin, like others, maintains that this mode of argument is clearly discernible in *On Liberty*. (Dworkin also recognizes a utilitarian line of argument in *On Liberty*. Like Berlin, Dworkin points out that the plausibility of Mill's utilitarian argument is contingent upon the empirical evidence. It is clear that Dworkin, like the utilitarians Stephen and Hart, does not think that the evidence supports Mill's general prohibition against paternalism. Also bear in mind here Berlin's claim that it is not Mill's utilitarianism but rather his very deep concern about the capacity for free choice that is at the heart of Mill's view.) That Mill places an absolute value upon free choice is reflected in passages such as this: "If a person possesses any tolerable amount of common sense and experience, his own mode of laying out his existence is the best, *not because it is the best in itself, but because it is his own mode*" (122, editor's emphasis). This line of reasoning, Dworkin argues, is also clearly seen in Mill's refusal to allow an individual to sell himself into slavery. Mill recognizes this important and unique exception to his general prohibition against paternalism precisely because selling oneself into slavery undermines the individual's freedom to make future choices. But, Dworkin asks, if paternalism is justified in this case because it is necessary to preserve the person's liberty to make future choices, why aren't *any such measures* likewise justified? Dworkin concludes that they are.

Endnotes

1. Carla Power. "The Lost Generation," *Newsweek*. Aug. 7, 2005.
2. "The Avuncular State: A Smarter, Softer Kind of Paternalism is Coming into Style," *The Economist*. April 6, 2006.
3. *Autobiography*, CW I: 259. ("CW" refers to *The Collected Works of John Stuart Mill*. The reference indicates volume and page number.)
4. In addition to Mill, the major philosophical proponents of liberalism include: John Locke (1632-1704), Immanuel Kant (1724-1804), Jeremy Bentham (1748-1832), Benjamin Constant (1767-1830), Wilhelm von Humboldt (1767-1835), L.T. Hobhouse (1864-1929), and, more recently, Isaiah Berlin (1909-97), H.L.A. Hart (1907-93), John Rawls (1921-2002), Robert Nozick (1938-2002), Ronald Dworkin (1931-), and Brian Barry (1936-).
5. *Autobiography*, CW I: 5.
6. *Autobiography*, CW I: 169, 171.
7. In addition to Mill's autobiography, see the biographies by Nicholas Capaldi and Michael St. John Packe. Alan Ryan's *The Philosophy of John Stuart Mill* and John Skorupski's *John Stuart Mill* are comprehensive accounts of Mill's philosophy.
8. Alexander Bain's *James Mill: A Biography* remains the standard biography.
9. John Mill himself recognized that his father's reputation would always be overshadowed by Bentham's. Reflecting on his father's intellectual legacy, he writes, "the thought of him merges too much in the deservedly superior fame of Bentham. Yet he was anything but Bentham's mere follower or disciple....he was himself one of the most original thinkers of his time." *Autobiography*, CW I: 211, 213.
10. See W.E.S. Thomas's *The Philosophical Radicals*.
11. As John Mill would later put it, "The present wretched education, and wretched social arrangements, are the only real hindrance to [happiness's] being attainable by almost all." *Utilitarianism*, CW X: 215.
12. *The Works of Jeremy Bentham* X: 473.
13. *Autobiography*, CW I: 69.
14. *Autobiography*, CW I: 137, 139.
15. *Autobiography*, CW I: 51.
16. Freudian interpreters have made much of the fact that the scene from Marmontel that so affected Mill is the father's death scene.
17. Commentators have pointed out that the three-part structure of Mill's autobiography—an extended account of his early development, a central period of emotional crisis, and a final period of recovery—mirrors Wordsworth's own autobiographical poem *The Prelude* (1850).
18. *Autobiography*, CW I: 151.
19. *Autobiography*, CW I: 169, 171.
20. *Autobiography*, CW I: 169. Mill's emphasis.
21. *Autobiography*, CW vol. 1, p. 213.
22. *Autobiography*, CW I: 163.
23. *Autobiography*, CW I: 169.
24. *Democracy in America*, vol. I, p. 263-4, 267.

25. Moral intuitionism should not be confused with the moral sentimentalism or moral sense theory of Francis Hutcheson (1694-1746) and David Hume (1711-76). Though both theories refer to a "moral sense," intuitionists maintain that the properties "perceived" by the moral sense are unique kinds of non-natural properties, whereas Hutcheson and Hume believe that the moral properties affecting the moral sense are ordinary empirical properties.
26. *Autobiography*, CW I: 233.
27. See, for example, "Remarks on Bentham" (1833), "Sedgwick's Discourse" (1835), and "Whewell on Moral Philosophy" (1852) in CW X.
28. *Autobiography*, CW I: 175.
29. See Jo Ellen Jacob's biography *The Voice of Harriet Taylor Mill*. A classic account of the relationship between John Mill and Harriet Taylor is F.A. Hayek's *John Stuart Mill and Harriet Taylor: Their Friendship and Subsequent Marriage*.
30. CW I: 182. Carlyle did not agree with Mill's assessment. He said, "She was full of unwise intellect, asking and re-asking stupid questions." (See Packe, 315).
31. After a perceived slight from Mill's mother the couple broke off all relations with her, and she is almost completely absence from Mill's autobiography.
32. CW XIV: 141-2. Pemmican is a food of the Native North Americans. It is a cake consisting of pounded dried meat mixed in a paste with melted fat and dried berries or fruits. Figuratively, 'pemmican' refers to extremely condensed writing.
33. *Autobiography*, CW I: 251.
34. *Autobiography*, CW I: 249, 257, 259.
35. Jo Ellen Jacobs defends Mill's account of Harriet Taylor's influence and contribution in her introduction to the *Complete Works of Harriet Taylor Mill* and *The Voice of Harriet Taylor Mill*. H.O. Pappe, on the other hand, contends in *John Stuart Mill and the Harriet Taylor Mill Myth* that Taylor's influence was negligible. In *On Liberty and Liberalism: The Case of John Stuart Mill*, Gertrude Himmelfarb argues that Harriet Taylor did exercise considerable influence over Mill—much for the worse, since she persuaded him to adopt more radical and less tenable positions than he otherwise would have.
36. See, for example, Isaiah Berlin's "John Stuart Mill and the Ends of Life" reprinted in *Four Essays on Liberty*.
37. See, for example, the work of Gray, Rees, Ryan, and Ten.
38. *Works* I: 1.
39. *Works* II: 253.
40. *Utilitarianism*, CW X: 210.
41. *Utilitarianism*, CW X: 210.
42. *Utilitarianism*, CW X: 210.
43. *Utilitarianism*, CW X: 211.
44. *Utilitarianism*, CW X: 211.
45. *Utilitarianism*, CW X: 212.
46. *Utilitarianism*, CW X: 235.
47. *Utilitarianism*, CW X: 224.
48. *Utilitarianism*, CW X: 224, 225.
49. His remarks about secondary or subordinate morals rules have led some commentators to argue that Mill should be understood as an advocate of *rule*-utilitarianism as opposed to *act*-utilitarianism. According to the act utilitarian the moral rightness or wrongness of an action is determined directly by its consequences—an action is morally right just in case its consequences are, on balance, better for all than any alternative action. The rule-utilitarian does not consider the consequences of each particular action but considers the consequences of adopting some general rule, such as "Tell the truth." The rule-utilitarian tells us to follow a rule if the consequences of adopting it are better, on balance, than the consequences of adopting an alternative rule. So, according to a rule-utilitarian, an action is morally right just in case it corresponds to a rule the general adoption of which has better consequences for all than any alternative

rule. The classic interpretation of Mill as a rule-utilitarian is J.O. Urmson's "The Interpretation of the Moral Philosophy of J.S. Mill" *Philosophical Quarterly*. 1953: 3.
50. *Utilitarianism*, *CW* X: 240.
51. *Utilitarianism*, *CW* X: 240. This, Mill thinks, is the fallacy underlying intuitionism generally.
52. *Utilitarianism*, *CW* X: 250, 251.
53. *Utilitarianism*, *CW* X: 255.
54. *Utilitarianism*, *CW* X: 250.
55. "Two Concepts of Liberty" reprinted in *Four Essays on Liberty*. "Positive freedom," by contrast, consists in self-mastery—that is, being under one's own rational control. Such self-mastery involves pursuing ends that one has freely and reflectively chosen, rather than pursuing the desires that one simply happens to have.
56. *Works* II: 501.
57. *Schenck v. United States*, 249 U.S. 47 (1919), p. 52. Charles Schenck and other members of the Socialist party were prosecuted under the Espionage Act of 1917 for distributing antiwar and antidraft pamphlets. The Court unanimously upheld the Espionage Act on the basis of Holmes's test.
58. See the chapter "*On Liberty* and Its Early Critics" in Rees's *John Stuart Mill's On Liberty*, and Nicholson's "The Reception and Early Reputation of Mill's Political Thought" in *The Cambridge Companion to Mill*.
59. *New Letters of Thomas Carlyle*, vol. II, p. 196.
60. *Liberty, Equality, Fraternity* p. 28, 66.
61. "The Principle of Liberty," reprinted as chapter V, in *John Stuart Mill's On Liberty*.
62. Regarding the application Mill's view to pornography, see Dyzenhaus's "John Stuart Mill and the Harm of Pornography" and Skipper's "Mill and Pornography" both reprinted in *Mill's On Liberty*. For a Millian approach to hate speech, see Brink's "Millian Principles, Freedom of Expression, and Hate Speech."
63. See Devlin's *The Enforcement of Morals* (much of which was published prior to the book in 1965).
64. Himmelfarb (1974) p. 30.
65. *The English Utilitarians*, vol. III, p. 244 n.1. In his biography of his brother, *The Life of Sir James Fitzjames Stephen* (1895), Leslie Stephen quotes from a letter that his brother sent to him: "I am falling foul of John Mill in his modern and more humane mood—or rather, I should say, in his sentimental mood—which always makes me feel that he is a deserter from the proper principles of rigidity and ferocity in which he was brought up" (308).
66. *Liberty, Equality, Fraternity*, p. 28-9.
67. "John Stuart Mill and the Ends of Life" in *Four Essays on Liberty*, p. 191.
68. *Ibid*. p. 192.
69. *Liberty, Equality, Fraternity*, p. 81.
70. *Ibid*. p. 67-8.
71. p. 32-3.
72. "Paternalism" reprinted in *Mill's On Liberty*, p. 75.
73. *Ibid*. p. 81.

BIBLIOGRAPHY

John Stuart Mill's Principal Works

A System of Logic, 2 vols. (1843).
Principles of Political Economy, 2 vols. (1848).
On Liberty. (1859).

Thoughts on Parliamentary Reform. (1859).
Essay on Representative Government. (1861).
Utilitarianism. (first printed in *Fraser's Magazine*, Oct.-Dec. 1861).
The Subjection of Women. (1869).
Autobiography. (ed. by Harriet Taylor, 1879).

The standard critical edition of Mill's works is: *The Collected Works of John Stuart Mill*, 33 vols. Gen. Ed. John Robson. (Toronto: Toronto University Press, 1963-1991.)

Books and Articles about Mill and His Philosophy in General

Capaldi, Nicholas. *John Stuart Mill: A Biography.* (Cambridge: Cambridge University Press, 2004).
Hayek, F.A. *John Stuart Mill and Harriet Taylor: Their Friendship and Subsequent Marriage.* (London: Routledge, 1951).
Packe, Michael St. John. *The Life of John Stuart Mill.* (New York: Macmillan, 1954).
Ryan, Alan. *The Philosophy of John Stuart Mill.* (London and New York: Macmillan, 1970 and 1988).
—*J.S. Mill.* (London: Routledge, 1974).
Skorupski, John. *John Stuart Mill.* (London, Routledge, 1989).
—*The Cambridge Companion to Mill.* (Cambridge: Cambridge University Press, 1998).

Books and Articles about *On Liberty*

Berger, Fred. *Happiness, Justice and Freedom: The Moral and Political Philosophy of John Stuart Mill.* (Berkeley: University of California Press, 1984).
Berlin, Isaiah. *Two Concepts of Liberty.* (Oxford: Clarendon Press, 1958).
Dworkin, Gerald (ed.). *Mill's* On Liberty: *Critical Essays.* (New York: Rowman & Littlefield, 1997).
Gray, John. *Mill on Liberty: A Defence.* (London: Routledge, 1983, rev. ed. 1996).
Himmelfarb, Gertrude. *On Liberty and Liberalism: The Case of John Stuart Mill.* (New York: Alfred A. Knopf, 1974).
Pyle, Andrew, ed. *Liberty: Contemporary Responses to John Stuart Mill.* (Bristol: Thoemmes Press, 1994).

Rees, John. *John Stuart Mill's "On Liberty"*. G.L. Williams (ed.) (Oxford: Clarendon Press, 1985).

Riley, Jonathan. *Mill: On Liberty*. (London: Routledge, 1998).

Ten, C.L. *Mill On Liberty*. (Oxford: Oxford University Press, 1980).

Other Works Cited in the Editor's Introduction

Bentham, Jeremy. *Works*. John Bowring, ed. (New York: Russell & Russell, 1962).

Berlin, Isaiah. *Four Essays on Liberty*. New York: Oxford University Press, 1970).

Devlin, Patrick. *The Enforcement of Morals*. (Oxford: Oxford University Press, 1965).

Feinberg, Joel. *Harm to Others*. (Oxford: Oxford University Press, 1984).

Hart, H.L.A. *Law, Liberty, and Morality*. (New York: Random House, 1966).

Jacobs, Jo Ellen. *The Voice of Harriet Taylor Mill*. (Bloomington: Indiana University Press, 2002.)

Mill, Harriet Taylor. *Complete Works*. Jacobs and Payne, eds. (Bloomington: Indiana University Press, 1998.)

Pappe, H.O. *John Stuart Mill and the Harriet Taylor Mill Myth*. (Melbourne, 1960).

Stephen, James Fitzjames. *Liberty, Equality, Fraternity*. (Cambridge: Cambridge University Press, 1967).

Stephen, Leslie. *The English Utilitarians* (3 vols.) (London: Duckworth, 1900).

—*The Life of Sir James Fitzjames Stephen* (London, 1895).

A NOTE ON THE TEXT

Four editions of *On Liberty* were published in Mill's lifetime. The first and second editions were published by Parker in London in 1859. The third edition was published by Longman, Green, Longman, Roberts & Green in London in 1864, and the fourth edition—a reprint of the third—was published by Longmans, Green, Reader and Dyer in London in 1869. The present edition is based upon the fourth edition. The minor variations from earlier editions are noted. (The first edition is indicated by "1859a", and the second edition by "1859b".) The editor's explanatory notes are numbered. Spelling, punctuation, capitalization, and editorial style have been modified to conform to current American usage.

MICHAEL B. MATHIAS
Union College
Schenectady, New York
October 2006

Domain of consciense - thought + opinion
planning of life - taste + pursuits
Uniting w/o harming others

John Stuart Mill

On Liberty

*The grand, leading principle, towards which every argument unfolded
in these pages directly converges, is the absolute and essential
importance of human development in its richest diversity.*

—WILHELM VON HUMBOLDT,
Sphere and Duties of Government.[1]

To the beloved and deplored memory of her[1] who was the inspirer, and
in part the author, of all that is best in my writings—the friend and wife
whose exalted sense of truth and right was my strongest incitement, and
whose approbation was my chief reward—I dedicate this volume. Like
all that I have written for many years, it belongs as much to her as to me;
but the work as it stands has had, in a very insufficient degree, the inestimable advantage of her revision; some of the most important portions
having been reserved for a more careful reexamination which they are
now never destined to receive. Were I but capable of interpreting to the
world one half the great thoughts and noble feelings which are buried in
her grave, I should be the medium of a greater benefit to it than is ever
likely to arise from anything that I can write unprompted and unassisted
by her all but unrivalled wisdom.

On Liberty

CHAPTER I

Introductory

THE subject of this essay is not the so-called liberty of the will, so unfortunately opposed to the misnamed doctrine of philosophical necessity;[1] but civil, or social liberty: the nature and limits of the power which can be legitimately exercised by society over the individual. A question seldom stated, and hardly ever discussed in general terms, but which profoundly influences the practical controversies of the age by its latent presence, and is likely soon to make itself recognized as the vital question of the future. It is so far from being new that, in a certain sense, it has divided mankind almost from the remotest ages; but in the stage of progress into which the more civilized portions of the species have now entered, it presents itself under new conditions and requires a different and more fundamental treatment.

The struggle between liberty and authority is the most conspicuous feature in the portions of history with which we are earliest familiar, particularly in that of Greece, Rome, and England. But in old times this contest was between subjects, or some classes of subjects, and the government. By *liberty* was meant protection against the tyranny of the political rulers. The rulers were conceived (except in some of the popular governments of Greece) as in a necessarily antagonistic position to the people whom they ruled. They consisted of a governing One, or a governing tribe or caste, who derived their authority from inheritance or

do something w/o being punished

conquest, who, at all events, did not hold it at the pleasure of the governed, and whose supremacy men did not venture, perhaps did not desire, to contest, whatever precautions might be taken against its oppressive exercise. Their power was regarded as necessary, but also as highly dangerous; as a weapon which they would attempt to use against their subjects, no less than against external enemies. To prevent the weaker members of the community from being preyed upon by innumerable vultures, it was needful that there should be an animal of prey stronger than the rest, commissioned to keep them down.[2] But as the king of the vultures would be no less bent upon preying upon the flock than any of the minor harpies, it was indispensable to be in a perpetual attitude of defense against his beak and claws. The aim, therefore, of patriots was to set limits to the power which the ruler should be suffered to exercise over the community; and this limitation was what they meant by *liberty*. It was attempted in two ways. First, by obtaining a recognition of certain immunities, called political liberties or rights, which it was to be regarded as a breach of duty in the ruler to infringe, and which, if he did infringe, specific resistance or general rebellion was held to be justifiable.[3] A second, and generally a later, expedient was the establishment of constitutional checks by which the consent of the community, or of a body of some sort, supposed to represent its interests, was made a necessary condition to some of the more important acts of the governing power. To the first of these modes of limitation, the ruling power, in most European countries, was compelled, more or less, to submit. It was not so with the second; and, to attain this, or when already in some degree possessed, to attain it more completely, became everywhere the principal object of the lovers of liberty. And so long as mankind were content to combat one enemy by another, and to be ruled by a master on condition of being guaranteed more or less efficaciously against his tyranny, they did not carry their aspirations beyond this point.

A time, however, came in the progress of human affairs, when men ceased to think it a necessity of nature that their governors should be an independent power opposed in interest to themselves. It appeared to them much better that the various magistrates of the state should be their tenants or delegates, revocable at their pleasure.[4] In that way alone, it seemed, could they have complete security that the powers of government would never be abused to their disadvantage. By degrees this new demand for elective and temporary rulers became the prominent object of the exertions of the popular party, wherever any such party existed, and superseded, to a considerable extent, the previous efforts to limit the

power of rulers. As the struggle proceeded for making the ruling power emanate from the periodical choice of the ruled, some persons began to think that too much importance had been attached to the limitation of the power itself. *That* (it might seem) was a resource against rulers whose interests were habitually opposed to those of the people. What was now wanted was that the rulers should be identified with the people, that their interest and will should be the interest and will of the nation.[5] The nation did not need to be protected against its own will. There was no fear of its tyrannizing over itself. Let the rulers be effectually responsible to it, promptly removable by it, and it could afford to trust them with power of which it could itself dictate the use to be made. Their power was but the nation's own power, concentrated and in a form convenient for exercise. This mode of thought, or rather perhaps of feeling, was common among the last generation of European liberalism, in the Continental section of which, it still apparently predominates.[6] Those who admit any limit to what a government may do, except in the case of such governments as they think ought not to exist, stand out as brilliant exceptions among the political thinkers of the Continent. A similar tone of sentiment might by this time have been prevalent in our own country if the circumstances which for a time encouraged it had continued unaltered.

But, in political and philosophical theories, as well as in persons, success discloses faults and infirmities which failure might have concealed from observation. The notion that the people have no need to limit their power over themselves might seem axiomatic when popular government was a thing only dreamed about, or read of as having existed at some distant period of the past. Neither was that notion necessarily disturbed by such temporary aberrations as those of the French Revolution, the worst of which were the work of an usurping few, and which, in any case, belonged, not to the permanent working of popular institutions, but to a sudden and convulsive outbreak against monarchical and aristocratic despotism.[7] In time, however, a democratic republic came to occupy a large portion of the earth's surface, and made itself felt as one of the most powerful members of the community of nations,[8] and elective and responsible government became subject to the observations and criticisms which wait upon a great existing fact. It was now perceived that such phrases as "self-government" and "the power of the people over themselves" do not express the true state of the case. The "people" who exercise the power are not always the same people with those over whom it is exercised; and the "self-government" spoken of is not the government of each by himself, but of each by all the rest. The *will of the people*, moreover, practically means the will of the most numerous or the most active *part* of the people—the majority, or those who succeed in making themselves accepted as the majority; the people, consequently, *may* desire to oppress a part of their number, and precautions are as much needed against this as against any other abuse of power. The limitation, therefore, of the power of government over individuals loses none of its importance when the holders of power are regularly accountable to the community, that is, to the strongest party therein. This view of things, recommending itself equally to the intelligence of thinkers and to the inclination of those important classes in European society to whose real or supposed interests democracy is adverse, has had no difficulty in establishing itself; and in political speculations "the tyranny of the majority"[9] is now generally included among the evils against which society requires to be on its guard.

Like other tyrannies, the tyranny of the majority was at first, and is still vulgarly, held in dread chiefly as operating through the acts of the public authorities.[10] But reflecting persons[11] perceived that when society is itself the tyrant—society collectively over the separate individuals who compose it—its means of tyrannizing are not restricted to the acts which it may do by the hands of its political functionaries. Society can and does execute its own mandates; and if it issues wrong mandates instead of right, or any mandates at all in things with which it ought not to meddle, it practices a social tyranny more formidable than many kinds of political oppression, since, though not usually upheld by such extreme penalties, it leaves fewer means of escape, penetrating much more deeply into the details of life and enslaving the soul itself. Protection, therefore, against the tyranny of the magistrate is not enough: there needs [to be] protection also against the tyranny of the prevailing opinion and feeling; against the tendency of society to impose, by other means than civil penalties, its own ideas and practices as rules of conduct on those who dissent from them, to fetter the development, and, if possible, prevent the formation of any individuality not in harmony with its ways and compel all characters to fashion themselves upon the model of its own. There is a limit to the legitimate interference of collective opinion with individual independence; and to find that limit, and maintain it against encroachment, is as indispensable to a good condition of human affairs as protection against political despotism.

But though this proposition is not likely to be contested in general terms, the practical question [of] where to place the limit—how to make

the fitting adjustment between individual independence and social control—is a subject on which nearly everything remains to be done. All that
makes existence valuable to anyone depends on the enforcement of
restraints upon the actions of other people. Some rules of conduct, therefore, must be imposed—by law in the first place, and by opinion on
many things which are not fit subjects for the operation of law. What
these rules should be is the principal question in human affairs; but, if we
except a few of the most obvious cases, it is one of those which least
progress has been made in resolving. No two ages, and scarcely any two
countries, have decided it alike; and the decision of one age or country is
a wonder to another. Yet the people of any given age and country no
more suspect any difficulty in it than if it were a subject on which
mankind had always been agreed. The rules which obtain among themselves appear to them self-evident and self-justifying. This all but universal illusion is one of the examples of the magical influence of custom,
which is not only, as the proverb says, a second nature, but is continually
mistaken for the first. The effect of custom in preventing any misgiving
respecting the rules of conduct which mankind impose on one another, is
all the more complete because the subject is one on which it is not generally considered necessary that reasons should be given, either by one person to others or by each to himself. People are accustomed to believe and
have been encouraged in the belief by some who aspire to the character
of philosophers, that their feelings on subjects of this nature are better
than reasons, and render reasons unnecessary.[12] The practical principle
which guides them to their opinions on the regulation of human conduct
is the feeling in each person's mind that everybody should be required to
act as he, and those with whom he sympathizes, would like them to act.
No one, indeed, acknowledges to himself that his standard of judgment
is his own liking; but an opinion on a point of conduct, not supported by
reasons, can only count as one person's preference; and if the reasons,
when given, are a mere appeal to a similar preference felt by other people, it is still only many people's liking instead of one. To an ordinary
man, however, his own preference, thus supported, is not only a perfectly
satisfactory reason, but the only one he generally has for any of his
notions of morality, taste, or propriety which are not expressly written in
his religious creed, and his chief guide in the interpretation even of that.
Men's opinions, accordingly, on what is laudable or blamable are
affected by all the multifarious causes which influence their wishes in
regard to the conduct of others, and which are as numerous as those
which determine their wishes on any other subject. Sometimes their rea-

son; at other times their prejudices or superstitions; often their social affections, not seldom their antisocial ones—their envy or jealousy, their arrogance or contemptuousness; but, most commonly, their desires or fears for themselves—their legitimate or illegitimate self-interest. Wherever there is an ascendant class, a large portion of the morality of the country emanates from its class interests and its feelings of class superiority. The morality between Spartans and Helots,[13] between planters and Negroes, between princes and subjects, between nobles and roturiers,[14] between men and women, has been for the most part the creation of these class interests and feelings; and the sentiments thus generated react in turn upon the moral feelings of the members of the ascendant class, in their relations among themselves. Where, on the other hand, a class, formerly ascendant, has lost its ascendancy, or where its ascendancy is unpopular, the prevailing moral sentiments frequently bear the impress of an impatient dislike of superiority. Another grand determining principle of the rules of conduct, both in act and forbearance, which have been enforced by law or opinion has been the servility of mankind towards the supposed preferences or aversions of their temporal masters or of their gods. This servility, though essentially selfish, is not hypocrisy; it gives rise to perfectly genuine sentiments of abhorrence; it made men burn magicians and heretics. Among so many baser influences, the general and obvious interests of society have, of course, had a share, and a large one, in the direction of the moral sentiments; less, however, as a matter of reason, and on their own account, than as a consequence of the sympathies and antipathies which grew out of them; and sympathies and antipathies which had little or nothing to do with the interests of society have made themselves felt in the establishment of moralities with quite as great force.

The likings and dislikings of society, or of some powerful portion of it, are thus the main thing which has practically determined the rules laid down for general observance under the penalties of law or opinion. And, in general, those who have been in advance of society in thought and feeling have left this condition of things unassailed in principle, however they may have come into conflict with it in some of its details. They have occupied themselves in inquiring what things society ought to like or dislike, rather than in questioning whether its likings or dislikings should be a law to individuals. They preferred endeavoring to alter the feelings of mankind on the particular points on which they were themselves heretical, rather than make common cause in defense of freedom with heretics generally. The only case in which the higher ground has been taken on principle and maintained with consistency, by any but an individual here and there, is that of religious belief: a case instructive in many ways, and not least so as forming a most striking instance of the fallibility of what is called the moral sense;[15] for the *odium theologicum*,[16] in a sincere bigot, is one of the most unequivocal cases of moral feeling. Those who first broke the yoke of what called itself the Universal Church[17] were in general as little willing to permit difference of religious opinion as that church itself. But when the heat of the conflict was over, without giving a complete victory to any party, and each church or sect was reduced to limit its hopes to retaining possession of the ground it already occupied, minorities, seeing that they had no chance of becoming majorities, were under the necessity of pleading to those whom they could not convert for permission to differ. It is accordingly on this battlefield, almost solely, that the rights of the individual against society have been asserted on broad grounds of principle, and the claim of society to exercise authority over dissentients[18] openly controverted. The great writers to whom the world owes what religious liberty it possesses have mostly asserted freedom of conscience as an indefeasible right and denied absolutely that a human being is accountable to others for his religious belief.[19] Yet so natural to mankind is intolerance in whatever they really care about that religious freedom has hardly anywhere been practically realized, except where religious indifference, which dislikes to have its peace disturbed by theological quarrels, has added its weight to the scale. In the minds of almost all religious persons, even in the most tolerant countries, the duty of toleration is admitted with tacit reserves. One person will bear with dissent in matters of church government, but not of dogma; another can tolerate everybody, short of a Papist or an Unitarian;[20] another, everyone who believes in revealed religion; a few extend their charity a little further, but stop at the belief in a God and in a future state. Wherever the sentiment of the majority is still genuine and intense, it is found to have abated little of its claim to be obeyed.

In England, from the peculiar circumstances of our political history, though the yoke of opinion is perhaps heavier, that of law is lighter than in most other countries of Europe; and there is considerable jealousy of direct interference by the legislative or the executive power with private conduct—not so much from any just regard for the independence of the individual as from the still subsisting habit of looking on the government as representing an opposite interest to the public. The majority have not yet learned to feel the power of the government their power, or its opinions their opinions. When they do so, individual liberty will prob-

ably be as much exposed to invasion from the government as it already is
from public opinion. But, as yet, there is a considerable amount of feeling ready to be called forth against any attempt of the law to control
individuals in things in which they have not up till now been accustomed
to be controlled by it; and this with very little discrimination as to
whether the matter is, or is not, within the legitimate sphere of legal control; insomuch that the feeling, highly salutary on the whole, is perhaps
quite as often misplaced as well grounded in the particular instances of
its application. There is, in fact, no recognized principle by which the
propriety or impropriety of government interference is customarily
tested. People decide according to their personal preferences. Some,
whenever they see any good to be done or evil to be remedied, would
willingly instigate the government to undertake the business, while others prefer to bear almost any amount of social evil, rather than add one
to the departments of human interests amenable to governmental control. And men range themselves on one or the other side in any particular
case according to this general direction of their sentiments; or according
to the degree of interest which they feel in the particular thing which it is
proposed that the government should do; or according to the belief they
entertain that the government would, or would not, do it in the manner
they prefer; but very rarely on account of any opinion to which they consistently adhere, as to what things are fit to be done by a government.
And it seems to me that in consequence of this absence of rule or principle, one side is at present as often wrong as the other; the interference of
government is, with about equal frequency, improperly invoked and
improperly condemned.

The object of this essay is to assert one very simple principle, as entitled to govern absolutely the dealings of society with the individual in the
way of compulsion and control, whether the means used are physical
force in the form of legal penalties or the moral coercion of public opinion. That principle is that the sole end for which mankind are warranted,
individually or collectively, in interfering with the liberty of action of any
of their number is self-protection. That the only purpose for which
power can be rightfully exercised over any member of a civilized community, against his will, is to prevent harm to others. His own good, either
physical or moral, is not a sufficient warrant. He cannot rightfully be
compelled to do or forbear because it will be better for him to do so,
because it will make him happier, because, in the opinions of others, to
do so would be wise, or even right. These are good reasons for remonstrating[21] with him, or reasoning with him, or persuading him, or

entreating him, but not for compelling him, or visiting him with any evil
in case he does otherwise. To justify that, the conduct from which it is
desired to deter him must be calculated to produce evil to someone else.
The only part of the conduct of anyone for which he is amenable to society is that which concerns others. In the part which merely concerns himself, his independence is, of right, absolute. Over himself, over his own
body and mind, the individual is sovereign.

It is, perhaps, hardly necessary to say that this doctrine is meant to
apply only to human beings in the maturity of their faculties. We are not
speaking of children or of young persons below the age which the law
may fix as that of manhood or womanhood. Those who are still in a
state to require being taken care of by others must be protected against
their own actions as well as against external injury. For the same reason
we may leave out of consideration those backward states of society in
which the race itself may be considered as in its nonage. The early difficulties in the way of spontaneous progress are so great that there is seldom any choice of means for overcoming them; and a ruler full of the
spirit of improvement is warranted in the use of any expedients that will
attain an end perhaps otherwise unattainable. Despotism is a legitimate
mode of government in dealing with barbarians, provided the end is their
improvement and the means justified by actually effecting that end. Liberty, as a principle, has no application to any state of things anterior to
the time when mankind have become capable of being improved by free
and equal discussion. Until then, there is nothing for them but implicit
obedience to an Akbar or a Charlemagne,[22] if they are so fortunate as to
find one. But as soon as mankind have attained the capacity of being
guided to their own improvement by conviction or persuasion (a period
long since reached in all nations with whom we need here concern ourselves), compulsion, either in the direct form or in that of pains and
penalties for non-compliance, is no longer admissible as a means to their
own good, and justifiable only for the security of others.

It is proper to state that I forego any advantage which could be
derived to my argument from the idea of abstract right as a thing independent of utility. I regard utility as the ultimate appeal on all ethical
questions; but it must be utility in the largest sense, grounded on the permanent interests of man as a progressive being.[23] Those interests, I contend, authorize the subjection of individual spontaneity to external
control only in respect to those actions of each which concern the interest of other people. If anyone does an act hurtful to others, there is a
primâ facie[24] case for punishing him by law or, where legal penalties are

only exception: if someone is a threat to others

not safely applicable, by general disapprobation. There are also many positive acts for the benefit of others which he may rightfully be compelled to perform, such as to give evidence in a court of justice, to bear his fair share in the common defense or in any other joint work necessary to the interest of the society of which he enjoys the protection, and to perform certain acts of individual beneficence, such as saving a fellow creature's life, or interposing to protect the defenseless against ill-usage—things which whenever it is obviously a man's duty to do, he may rightfully be made responsible to society for not doing. A person may cause evil to others not only by his actions but by his inaction, and in either case he is justly accountable to them for the injury. The latter case, it is true, requires a much more cautious exercise of compulsion than the former. To make anyone answerable for doing evil to others is the rule; to make him answerable for not preventing evil is, comparatively speaking, the exception. Yet there are many cases clear enough and grave enough to justify that exception. In all things which regard the external relations of the individual, he is *de jure*[25] amenable to those whose interests are concerned, and, if need be, to society as their protector. There are often good reasons for not holding him to the responsibility; but these reasons must arise from the special expediencies of the case: either because it is a kind of case in which he is on the whole likely to act better when left to his own discretion than when controlled in any way in which society have it in their power to control him, or because the attempt to exercise control would produce other evils, greater than those which it would prevent. When such reasons as these preclude the enforcement of responsibility, the conscience of the agent himself should step into the vacant judgment seat and protect those interests of others which have no external protection; judging himself all the more rigidly because the case does not admit of his being made accountable to the judgment of his fellow-creatures.

But there is a sphere of action in which society, as distinguished from the individual, has, if any, only an indirect interest: comprehending all that portion of a person's life and conduct which affects only himself, or, if it also affects others, only with their free, voluntary, and undeceived consent and participation. When I say *only himself*, I mean directly and in the first instance; for whatever affects himself may affect others through* himself—and the objection which may be grounded on this

---

* through-*through* (1859a, 1859b).

true freedom means pursuing one's own path in their own way as long as it doesn't prevent others from doing so.

contingency will receive consideration in the sequel. This, then, is the appropriate region of human liberty. It comprises, first, the inward domain of consciousness, demanding liberty of conscience in the most comprehensive sense, liberty of thought and feeling, absolute freedom of opinion and sentiment on all subjects, practical or speculative, scientific, moral, or theological. The liberty of expressing and publishing opinions may seem to fall under a different principle, since it belongs to that part of the conduct of an individual which concerns other people; but, being almost of as much importance as the liberty of thought itself, and resting in great part on the same reasons, is practically inseparable from it. Secondly, the principle requires liberty of tastes and pursuits, of framing the plan of our life to suit our own character, of doing as we like, subject to such consequences as may follow, without impediment from our fellow-creatures, so long as what we do does not harm them even though they should think our conduct foolish, perverse, or wrong. Thirdly, from this liberty of each individual follows the liberty, within the same limits, of combination among individuals; freedom to unite for any purpose not involving harm to others—the persons combining being supposed to be of full age and not forced or deceived.

No society in which these liberties are not, on the whole, respected is free, whatever may be its form of government; and none is completely free in which they do not exist absolute and unqualified. The only freedom which deserves the name is that of pursuing our own good in our own way, so long as we do not attempt to deprive others of theirs or impede their efforts to obtain it. Each is the proper guardian of his own health, whether bodily, or mental and spiritual. Mankind are greater gainers by suffering each other to live as seems good to themselves than by compelling each to live as seems good to the rest.

Though this doctrine is anything but new and, to some persons, may have the air of a truism, there is no doctrine which stands more directly opposed to the general tendency of existing opinion and practice. Society has expended fully as much effort in the attempt (according to its lights) to compel people to conform to its notions of personal as of social excellence. The ancient commonwealths thought themselves entitled to practice, and the ancient philosophers countenanced, the regulation of every part of private conduct by public authority, on the ground that the state had a deep interest in the whole bodily and mental discipline of every one of its citizens—a mode of thinking which may have been admissible in small republics surrounded by powerful enemies, in constant peril of being subverted by foreign attack or internal commotion, and to which

threat
↳ unless

even a short interval of relaxed energy and self-command might so easily be fatal that they could not afford to wait for the salutary permanent effects of freedom. In the modern world, the greater size of political communities and, above all, the separation between the spiritual and temporal authority (which placed the direction of men's consciences in other hands than those which controlled their worldly affairs) prevented so great an interference by law in the details of private life; but the engines of moral repression have been wielded more strenuously against divergence from the reigning opinion in self-regarding than even in social matters; religion, the most powerful of the elements which have entered into the formation of moral feeling, having almost always been governed either by the ambition of a hierarchy seeking control over every department of human conduct, or by the spirit of Puritanism.[26] And some of those modern reformers who have placed themselves in strongest opposition to the religions of the past have been no way behind either churches or sects in their assertion of the right of spiritual domination: M. Comte, in particular, whose social system, as unfolded in his *Système* de Politique Positive*, aims at establishing (though by moral more than by legal appliances) a despotism of society over the individual surpassing anything contemplated in the political ideal of the most rigid disciplinarian among the ancient philosophers.[27]

Apart from the peculiar tenets of individual thinkers, there is also in the world at large an increasing inclination to stretch unduly the powers of society over the individual, both by the force of opinion and even by that of legislation; and as the tendency of all the changes taking place in the world is to strengthen society and diminish the power of the individual, this encroachment is not one of the evils which tend spontaneously to disappear, but, on the contrary, to grow more and more formidable. The disposition of mankind, whether as rulers or as fellow-citizens, to impose their own opinions and inclinations as a rule of conduct on others is so energetically supported by some of the best and by some of the worst feelings incident to human nature that it is hardly ever kept under restraint by anything but want of power; and as the power is not declining, but growing, unless a strong barrier of moral conviction can be raised against the mischief, we must expect, in the present circumstances of the world, to see it increase.

moral conviction against the conformity tendency arises.

---

* Système-Traité (1859a, 1859b).

It will be convenient for the argument if, instead of at once entering upon the general thesis, we confine ourselves in the first instance to a single branch of it, on which the principle here stated is, if not fully, yet to a certain point, recognized by the current opinions. This one branch is the *liberty of thought*, from which it is impossible to separate the cognate liberty of speaking and of writing. Although these liberties, to some considerable amount, form part of the political morality of all countries which profess religious toleration and free institutions, the grounds, both philosophical and practical, on which they rest are perhaps not so familiar to the general mind, nor so thoroughly appreciated by many even of the leaders of opinion, as might have been expected. Those grounds, when rightly understood, are of much wider application than to only one division of the subject, and a thorough consideration of this part of the question will be found the best introduction to the remainder. Those to whom nothing which I am about to say will be new may therefore, I hope, excuse me if on a subject which for now three centuries has been so often discussed, I venture on one discussion more.

CHAPTER II

Of the Liberty of Thought and Discussion

THE time, it is to be hoped, is gone by when any defense would be necessary of the "liberty of the press" as one of the securities against corrupt or tyrannical government. No argument, we may suppose, can now be needed against permitting a legislature or an executive, not identified in interest with the people, to prescribe opinions to them and determine what doctrines or what arguments they shall be allowed to hear. This aspect of the question, besides, has been so often and so triumphantly enforced by preceding writers that it needs not be specially insisted on in this place. Though the law of England, on the subject of the press, is as servile to this day as it was in the time of the Tudors,[1] there is little danger of its being actually put in force against political discussion except during some temporary panic when fear of insurrection drives ministers and judges from their propriety;* and,

---

* These words had scarcely been written when, as if to give them an emphatic contradiction, occurred the Government Press Prosecutions of 1858. That ill-judged interference with the liberty of public discussion has not, however, induced me to alter a single word in the text, nor has it at all weakened my conviction that, moments of panic excepted, the era of pains and penalties for political discussion has, in our own country, passed away. For, in the first place, the prosecutions were not persisted in; and, in the second, they were never, properly speaking, political prosecutions. The offense charged was not that of criticizing institutions or the acts or persons of rulers, but of circulating what was deemed an immoral doctrine, the lawfulness of tyrannicide. [Editor: Tyrannicide is the killing or assassination of a tyrant. Mill is referring to the prosecution of the London publisher Edward Truelove, who published W.E. Adams's pamphlet titled "Tyrannicide: Is it Justifiable?" which defended an attempt by the Italian revolutionary Felice Orsini to assassinate Napoleon III.]

speaking generally, it is not, in constitutional countries, to be apprehended that the government, whether completely responsible to the
people or not, will often attempt to control the expression of opinion,
except when in doing so it makes itself the organ of the general intolerance of the public. Let us suppose, therefore, that the government is
entirely at one with the people, and never thinks of exerting any power
of coercion unless in agreement with what it conceives to be their voice.
But I deny the right of the people to exercise such coercion, either by
themselves or by their government. The power itself is illegitimate. The
best government has no more title to it than the worst. It is as noxious,
or more noxious, when exerted in accordance with public opinion than
when in opposition to it. If all mankind minus one were of one opinion,
and only one person were of the contrary opinion, mankind would be
no more justified in silencing that one person than he, if he had the
power, would be justified in silencing mankind. Were an opinion a personal possession of no value except to the owner, if to be obstructed in
the enjoyment of it were simply a private injury, it would make some
difference whether the injury was inflicted only on a few persons or on
many. But the peculiar evil of silencing the expression of an opinion is
that it is robbing the human race, posterity as well as the existing generation—those who dissent from the opinion, still more than those who
hold it. If the opinion is right, they are deprived of the opportunity of
exchanging error for truth; if wrong, they lose, what is almost as great
a benefit, the clearer perception and livelier impression of truth produced by its collision with error.
    It is necessary to consider separately these two hypotheses, each of
which has a distinct branch of the argument corresponding to it. We can

---

If the arguments of the present chapter are of any validity, there ought to exist the
fullest liberty of professing and discussing, as a matter of ethical conviction, any doctrine,
however immoral it may be considered. It would, therefore, be irrelevant and out of place
to examine here whether the doctrine of tyrannicide deserves that title. I shall content
myself with saying that the subject has been at all times one of the open questions of
morals; that the act of a private citizen in striking down a criminal—who, by raising himself above the law, has placed himself beyond the reach of legal punishment or control—has
been accounted by whole nations, and by some of the best and wisest of men, not a crime
but an act of exalted virtue; and that, right or wrong, it is not of the nature of assassination,
but of civil war. As such, I hold that the instigation to it, in a specific case, may be a proper
subject of punishment, but only if an overt act has followed, and at least a probable connection can be established between the act and the instigation. Even then it is not a foreign
government, but the very government assailed, which alone, in the exercise of self-defense,
can legitimately punish attacks directed against its own existence.

never be sure that the opinion we are endeavoring to stifle is a false opinion; and if we were sure, stifling it would be an evil still.

First, the opinion which it is attempted to suppress by authority may possibly be true. Those who desire to suppress it, of course, deny its truth; but they are not infallible. They have no authority to decide the question for all mankind and exclude every other person from the means of judging. To refuse a hearing to an opinion because they are sure that it is false is to assume that *their* certainty is the same thing as *absolute* certainty. All silencing of discussion is an assumption of infallibility. Its condemnation may be allowed to rest on this common argument, not the worse for being common.

Unfortunately for the good sense of mankind, the fact of their fallibility is far from carrying the weight in their practical judgment which is always allowed to it in theory; for while everyone well knows himself to be fallible, few think it necessary to take any precautions against their own fallibility, or admit the supposition that any opinion of which they feel very certain may be one of the examples of the error to which they acknowledge themselves to be liable. Absolute princes, or others who are accustomed to unlimited deference, usually feel this complete confidence in their own opinions on nearly all subjects. People more happily situated, who sometimes hear their opinions disputed and are not wholly unused to being set right when they are wrong, place the same unbounded reliance only on such of their opinions as are shared by all who surround them, or to whom they habitually defer; for in proportion to a man's want of confidence in his own solitary judgment does he usually repose, with implicit trust, on the infallibility of "the world" in general. And *the world*, to each individual, means the part of it with which he comes in contact: his party, his sect, his church, his class of society; the man may be called, by comparison, almost liberal and large-minded to whom it means anything so comprehensive as his own country or his own age. Nor is his faith in this collective authority at all shaken by his being aware that other ages, countries, sects, churches, classes, and parties have thought, and even now think, the exact reverse. He devolves upon his own world the responsibility of being in the right against the dissentient worlds of other people; and it never troubles him that mere accident has decided which of these numerous worlds is the object of his reliance, and that the same causes which make him a Churchman in London would have made him a Buddhist or a Confucian in Peking.[2] Yet it is as evident in itself, as any amount of argument can make it, that ages are no more infallible than individuals—every age having held many opinions which subsequent ages have deemed not only false but absurd; and it is as certain that many opinions, now general, will be rejected by future ages, as it is that many, once general, are rejected by the present.

The objection likely to be made to this argument would probably take some such form as the following. There is no greater assumption of infallibility in forbidding the propagation of error than in any other thing which is done by public authority on its own judgment and responsibility. Judgment is given to men that they may use it. Because it may be used erroneously, are men to be told that they ought not to use it at all? To prohibit what they think pernicious is not claiming exemption from error, but fulfilling the duty incumbent on them, although fallible, of acting on their conscientious conviction. If we were never to act on our opinions, because those opinions may be wrong, we should leave all our interests uncared for, and all our duties unperformed. An objection which applies to all conduct can be no valid objection to any conduct in particular. It is the duty of governments, and of individuals, to form the truest opinions they can; to form them carefully, and never impose them upon others unless they are quite sure of being right. But when they are sure (such reasoners may say), it is not conscientiousness but cowardice to shrink from acting on their opinions and allow doctrines which they honestly think dangerous to the welfare of mankind, either in this life or in another, to be scattered abroad without restraint, because other people, in less enlightened times, have persecuted opinions now believed to be true. Let us take care, it may be said, not to make the same mistake; but governments and nations have made mistakes in other things which are not denied to be fit subjects for the exercise of authority: they have laid on bad taxes, made unjust wars. Ought we therefore to lay on no taxes and, under whatever provocation, make no wars? Men and governments must act to the best of their ability. There is no such thing as absolute certainty, but there is assurance sufficient for the purposes of human life. We may, and must, assume our opinion to be true for the guidance of our own conduct; and it is assuming no more when we forbid bad men to pervert society by the propagation of opinions which we regard as false and pernicious.

I answer that it is assuming very much more. There is the greatest difference between presuming an opinion to be true because, with every opportunity for contesting it, it has not been refuted, and assuming its truth for the purpose of not permitting its refutation. Complete liberty of contradicting and disproving our opinion is the very condition which justifies us in assuming its truth for purposes of action; and on no other

human judgment is valuable when people remain open to criticism. We can correct our mistakes through experience & discussion. - also used to refute 2nd criticism (pg 82).

terms can a being with human faculties have any rational assurance of being right.

When we consider either the history of opinion or the ordinary conduct of human life, to what is it to be ascribed that the one and the other are no worse than they are? Not certainly to the inherent force of the human understanding, for on any matter not self-evident there are ninety-nine persons totally incapable of judging of it for one who is capable; and the capacity of the hundredth person is only comparative, for the majority of the eminent men of every past generation held many opinions now known to be erroneous, and did or approved numerous things which no one will now justify. Why is it, then, that there is on the whole a preponderance among mankind of rational opinions and rational conduct? If there really is this preponderance—which there must be unless human affairs are, and have always been, in an almost desperate state—it is owing to a quality of the human mind, the source of everything respectable in man either as an intellectual or as a moral being, namely, that his errors are corrigible. He is capable of rectifying his mistakes by discussion and experience. Not by experience alone. There must be discussion to show how experience is to be interpreted. Wrong opinions and practices gradually yield to fact and argument; but facts and arguments, to produce any effect on the mind, must be brought before it. Very few facts are able to tell their own story without comments to bring out their meaning. The whole strength and value, then, of human judgment depending on the one property, that it can be set right when it is wrong, reliance can be placed on it only when the means of setting it right are kept constantly at hand. In the case of any person whose judgment is really deserving of confidence, how has it become so? Because he has kept his mind open to criticism of his opinions and conduct. Because it has been his practice to listen to all that could be said against him; to profit by as much of it as was just, and expound to himself, and upon occasion to others, the fallacy of what was fallacious. Because he has felt that the only way in which a human being can make some approach to knowing the whole of a subject is by hearing what can be said about it by persons of every variety of opinion, and studying all modes in which it can be looked at by every character of mind. No wise man ever acquired his wisdom in any mode but this; nor is it in the nature of human intellect to become wise in any other manner. The steady habit of correcting and completing his own opinion by collating it with those of others, so far from causing doubt and hesitation in carrying it into practice, is the only stable foundation for a just reliance on it; for, being cognizant of all that can, at least obviously, be said against him, and having taken up his position against all gainsay-ers[3]—knowing that he has sought for objections and difficulties instead of avoiding them, and has shut out no light which can be thrown upon the subject from any quarter—he has a right to think his judgment bet-ter than that of any person, or any multitude, who have not gone through a similar process.

It is not too much to require that what the wisest of mankind, those who are best entitled to trust their own judgment, find necessary to war-rant their relying on it should be submitted to by that miscellaneous col-lection of a few wise and many foolish individuals called the public. The most intolerant of churches, the Roman Catholic Church, even at the canonization of a saint, admits, and listens patiently to, a "devil's advo-cate."[4] The holiest of men, it appears, cannot be admitted to posthu-mous honors until all that the devil could say against him is known and weighed. If even the Newtonian philosophy[5] were not permitted to be questioned, mankind could not feel as complete assurance of its truth as they now do. The beliefs which we have most warrant for have no safe-guard to rest on, but a standing invitation to the whole world to prove them unfounded. If the challenge is not accepted, or is accepted and the attempt fails, we are far enough from certainty still, but we have done the best that the existing state of human reason admits of—we have neg-lected nothing that could give the truth a chance of reaching us; if the lists are kept open, we may hope that if there is a better truth, it will be found when the human mind is capable of receiving it; and in the mean-time we may rely on having attained such approach to truth as is possible in our own day. This is the amount of certainty attainable by a fallible being, and this the sole way of attaining it.

Strange it is that men should admit the validity of the arguments for free discussion, but object to their being "pushed to an extreme," not seeing that unless the reasons are good for an extreme case, they are not good for any case. Strange that they should imagine that they are not assuming infallibility when they acknowledge that there should be free discussion on all subjects which can possibly be *doubtful*, but think that some particular principle or doctrine should be forbidden to be ques-tioned because it is so* *certain*, that is, because *they are certain* that it is certain. To call any proposition certain, while there is anyone who would

---

* so—*so* (1959a, 1859b).

deny its certainty if permitted, but who is not permitted, is to assume that we ourselves, and those who agree with us, are the judges of certainty, and judges without hearing the other side.

In the present age, which has been described as "destitute of faith, but terrified at skepticism"[6]—in which people feel sure, not so much that their opinions are true, as that they should not know what to do without them—the claims of an opinion to be protected from public attack are rested not so much on its truth as on its importance to society. There are, it is alleged, certain beliefs so useful, not to say indispensable, to well-being that it is as much the duty of governments to uphold those beliefs as to protect any other of the interests of society. In a case of such necessity, and so directly in the line of their duty, something less than infallibility may, it is maintained, warrant, and even bind, governments to act on their own opinion confirmed by the general opinion of mankind. It is also often argued, and still oftener thought, that none but bad men would desire to weaken these salutary beliefs; and there can be nothing wrong, it is thought, in restraining bad men and prohibiting what only such men would wish to practice. This mode of thinking makes the justification of restraints on discussion not a question of the truth of doctrines but of their usefulness, and flatters itself by that means to escape the responsibility of claiming to be an infallible judge of opinions. But those who thus satisfy themselves do not perceive that the assumption of infallibility is merely shifted from one point to another. The usefulness of an opinion is itself [a] matter of opinion—as disputable, as open to discussion, and requiring discussion as much as the opinion itself. There is the same need of an infallible judge of opinions to decide an opinion to be noxious, as to decide it to be false, unless the opinion condemned has full opportunity of defending itself. And it will not do to say that the heretic may be allowed to maintain the utility or harmlessness of his opinion, though forbidden to maintain its truth. The truth of an opinion is part of its utility. If we would know whether or not it is desirable that a proposition should be believed, is it possible to exclude the consideration of whether or not it is true? In the opinion, not of bad men, but of the best men, no belief which is contrary to truth can be really useful—and can you prevent such men from urging that plea when they are charged with culpability for denying some doctrine which they are told is useful, but which they believe to be false? Those who are on the side of received opinions never fail to take all possible advantage of this plea; you do not find *them* handling the question of utility as if it could be completely abstracted from that of truth; on the contrary, it is, above all, because their doctrine is the "truth"* that the knowledge or the belief of it is held to be so indispensable. There can be no fair discussion of the question of usefulness when an argument so vital may be employed on one side, but not on the other. And in point of fact, when law or public feeling do not permit the truth of an opinion to be disputed, they are just as little tolerant of a denial of its usefulness. The utmost they allow is an extenuation of its absolute necessity, or of the positive guilt of rejecting it.

In order more fully to illustrate the mischief of denying a hearing to opinions because we, in our own judgment, have condemned them, it will be desirable to fix down the discussion to a concrete case; and I choose, by preference, the cases which are least favorable to me—in which the argument against freedom of opinion, both on the score of truth and on that of utility, is considered the strongest. Let the opinions impugned be the belief in a God and in a future state, or any of the commonly received doctrines of morality. To fight the battle on such ground gives a great advantage to an unfair antagonist, since he will be sure to say (and many who have no desire to be unfair will say it internally), "Are these the doctrines which you do not deem sufficiently certain to be taken under the protection of law? Is the belief in a God one of the opinions, to feel sure of which, you hold to be assuming infallibility?" But I must be permitted to observe that it is not the feeling sure of a doctrine (be it what it may) which I call an assumption of infallibility. It is the undertaking to decide that question *for others*, without allowing them to hear what can be said on the contrary side. And I denounce and reprobate this pretension not the less if put forth on the side of my most solemn convictions. However positive anyone's persuasion may be, not only of the falsity, but of the pernicious consequences—not only of the pernicious consequences, but (to adopt expressions which I altogether condemn) the immorality and impiety of an opinion—yet if, in pursuance of that private judgment, though backed by the public judgment of his country or his cotemporaries, he prevents the opinion from being heard in its defense, he assumes infallibility. And so far from the assumption being less objectionable or less dangerous because the opinion is called immoral or impious, this is the case of all others in which it is most fatal. These are exactly the occasions on which the men of one generation commit those dreadful mistakes which excite the astonishment and horror of posterity. It is among such that we find the instances

---

* the "truth"—"the truth" (1859a, 1859b, 1864).

memorable in history, when the arm of the law has been employed to
root out the best men and the noblest doctrines; with deplorable success
as to the men, though some of the doctrines have survived to be (as if in
mockery) invoked in defense of similar conduct towards those who dissent from *them*, or from their received interpretation.

Mankind can hardly be too often reminded that there was once a man
named Socrates, between whom and the legal authorities and public
opinion of his time there took place a memorable collision.[7] Born in an
age and country abounding in individual greatness, this man has been
handed down to us by those who best knew both him and the age as the
most virtuous man in it; while we know him as the head and prototype
of all subsequent teachers of virtue, the source equally of the lofty inspi-
ration of Plato and the judicious utilitarianism of Aristotle, "*i maëstri di
color che sanno*,"[8] the two headsprings of ethical as of all other philosophy. This acknowledged master of all the eminent thinkers who have
since lived—whose fame, still growing after more than two thousand
years, all but outweighs the whole remainder of the names which make
his native city illustrious—was put to death by his countrymen after a
judicial conviction for impiety and immorality. Impiety, in denying the
gods recognized by the state; indeed, his accuser asserted (see the *Apolo-
gia*[9])that he believed in no gods at all. Immorality, in being, by his doctrines and instructions, a "corrupter of youth." Of these charges the
tribunal, there is every ground for believing, honestly found him guilty,
and condemned the man who probably of all then born had deserved
best of mankind to be put to death as a criminal.

To pass from this to the only other instance of judicial iniquity, the
mention of which, after the condemnation of Socrates, would not be an
anticlimax: the event which took place on Calvary[10] rather more than
eighteen hundred years ago. The man who left on the memory of those
who witnessed his life and conversation such an impression of his moral
grandeur that eighteen subsequent centuries have done homage to him as
the Almighty in person, was ignominiously put to death, as what? As a
blasphemer. Men did not merely mistake their benefactor; they mistook
him for the exact contrary of what he was and treated him as that
prodigy of impiety which they themselves are now held to be for their
treatment of him. The feelings with which mankind now regard these
lamentable transactions, especially the latter of the two, render them
extremely unjust in their judgment of the unhappy actors. These were, to
all appearance, not bad men—not worse than men most commonly are,
but rather the contrary; men who possessed in a full, or somewhat more

than a full measure, the religious, moral, and patriotic feelings of their time and people: the very kind of men who, in all times, our own included, have every chance of passing through life blameless and respected. The high-priest who rent his garments when the words were pronounced,[11] which, according to all the ideas of his country, constituted the blackest guilt, was in all probability quite as sincere in his horror and indignation as the generality of respectable and pious men now are in the religious and moral sentiments they profess; and most of those who now shudder at his conduct, if they had lived in his time and been born Jews, would have acted precisely as he did. Orthodox Christians who are tempted to think that those who stoned to death the first martyrs must have been worse men than they themselves are ought to remember that one of those persecutors was Saint Paul.[12]

Let us add one more example, the most striking of all, if the impressiveness of an error is measured by the wisdom and virtue of him who falls into it. If ever anyone possessed of power had grounds for thinking himself the best and most enlightened among his contemporaries, it was the Emperor Marcus Aurelius.[13] Absolute monarch of the whole civilized world, he preserved through life not only the most unblemished justice, but what was less to be expected from his Stoical breeding, the tenderest heart. The few failings which are attributed to him were all on the side of indulgence, while his writings, the highest ethical product of the ancient mind, differ scarcely perceptibly, if they differ at all, from the most characteristic teachings of Christ. This man, a better Christian in all but the dogmatic sense of the word than almost any of the ostensibly Christian sovereigns who have since reigned, persecuted Christianity. Placed at the summit of all the previous attainments of humanity, with an open, unfettered intellect, and a character which led him of himself to embody in his moral writings the Christian ideal, he yet failed to see that Christianity was to be a good and not an evil to the world, with his duties to which he was so deeply penetrated. Existing society he knew to be in a deplorable state. But such as it was, he saw, or thought he saw, that it was held together and prevented from being worse by belief and reverence of the received divinities. As a ruler of mankind, he deemed it his duty not to suffer society to fall in pieces; and saw not how, if its existing ties were removed, any others could be formed which could again knit it together. The new religion openly aimed at dissolving these ties; unless, therefore, it was his duty to adopt that religion, it seemed to be his duty to put it down. Inasmuch then as the theology of Christianity did not appear to him true or of divine origin, inasmuch as this strange history of a crucified God was not credible to him, and a system which purported to rest entirely upon a foundation to him so wholly unbelievable, could not be foreseen by him to be that renovating agency which, after all abatements, it has in fact proved to be—the gentlest and most amiable of philosophers and rulers, under a solemn sense of duty, authorized the persecution of Christianity. To my mind this is one of the most tragic facts in all history. It is a bitter thought how different a thing the Christianity of the world might have been if the Christian faith had been adopted as the religion of the empire under the auspices of Marcus Aurelius instead of those of Constantine.[14] But it would be equally unjust to him and false to truth to deny that no one plea which can be urged for punishing anti-Christian teaching was wanting to Marcus Aurelius for punishing, as he did, the propagation of Christianity. No Christian more firmly believes that atheism is false and tends to the dissolution of society than Marcus Aurelius believed the same things of Christianity; he who, of all men then living, might have been thought the most capable of appreciating it. Unless anyone who approves of punishment for the promulgation of opinions flatters himself that he is a wiser and better man than Marcus Aurelius—more deeply versed in the wisdom of his time, more elevated in his intellect above it, more earnest in his search for truth, or more single-minded in his devotion to it when found—let him abstain from that assumption of the joint infallibility of himself and the multitude which the great Antoninus made with so unfortunate a result.

Aware of the impossibility of defending the use of punishment for restraining irreligious opinions by any argument which will not justify Marcus Antoninus, the enemies of religious freedom, when hard pressed, occasionally accept this consequence, and say, with Dr. Johnson, that the persecutors of Christianity were in the right, that persecution is an ordeal through which truth ought to pass, and always passes successfully, legal penalties being, in the end, powerless against truth, though sometimes beneficially effective against mischievous errors.[15] This is a form of the argument for religious intolerance sufficiently remarkable not to be passed without notice.

A theory which maintains that truth may justifiably be persecuted because persecution cannot possibly do it any harm cannot be charged with being intentionally hostile to the reception of new truths; but we cannot commend the generosity of its dealing with the persons to whom mankind are indebted for them. To discover to the world something which deeply concerns it, and of which it was previously ignorant, to prove to it that it had been mistaken on some vital point of temporal or spiritual interest, is as important a service as a human being can render to his fellow creatures, and in certain cases, as in those of the early Christians and of the Reformers, those who think with Dr. Johnson believe it to have been the most precious gift which could be bestowed on mankind. That the authors of such splendid benefits should be requited by martyrdom, that their reward should be to be dealt with as the vilest of criminals, is not, upon this theory, a deplorable error and misfortune for which humanity should mourn in sackcloth and ashes, but the normal and justifiable state of things. The propounder of a new truth, according to this doctrine, should stand, as stood, in the legislation of the Locrians, the proposer of a new law, with a halter round his neck, to be instantly tightened if the public assembly did not, on hearing his reasons, then and there adopt his proposition.[16] People who defend this mode of treating benefactors cannot be supposed to set much value on the benefit; and I believe this view of the subject is mostly confined to the sort of persons who think that new truths may have been desirable once, but that we have had enough of them now.

But, indeed, the dictum that truth always triumphs over persecution is one of those pleasant falsehoods which men repeat after one another till they pass into commonplaces, but which all experience refutes. History teems with instances of truth put down by persecution. If not suppressed forever, it may be thrown back for centuries. To speak only of religious opinions: the Reformation broke out at least twenty times before Luther, and was put down. Arnold of Brescia was put down. Fra Dolcino was put down. Savonarola was put down. The Albigeois were put down. The Vaudois were put down. The Lollards were put down. The Hussites were put down.[17] Even after the era of Luther, wherever persecution was persisted in, it was successful. In Spain, Italy, Flanders, the Austrian empire, Protestantism was rooted out; and, most likely, would have been so in England, had Queen Mary lived or Queen Elizabeth died.[18] Persecution has always succeeded, save where the heretics were too strong a party to be effectually persecuted. No reasonable person can doubt that Christianity might have been extirpated in the Roman Empire. It spread and became predominant because the persecutions were only occasional, lasting but a short time, and separated by long intervals of almost undisturbed propagandism. It is a piece of idle sentimentality that truth, merely as truth, has any inherent power denied to error, of prevailing against the dungeon and the stake. Men are not more zealous for truth than they often are for error, and a sufficient application of legal or even of social penalties will generally succeed in stopping the propagation of either. The real advantage which truth has consists in this, that when an opinion is true, it may be extinguished once, twice, or many times, but in the course of ages there will generally be found persons to rediscover it, until some one of its reappearances falls on a time when from favorable circumstances it escapes persecution until it has made such head as to withstand all subsequent attempts to suppress it.

It will be said that we do not now put to death the introducers of new opinions: we are not like our fathers who slew the prophets, we even build sepulchers[19] to them. It is true we no longer put heretics to death, and the amount of penal infliction which modern feeling would probably tolerate, even against the most obnoxious opinions, is not sufficient to extirpate them. But let us not flatter ourselves that we are yet free from the stain even of legal persecution. Penalties for opinion, or at least for its expression, still exist by law; and their enforcement is not, even in these times, so unexampled as to make it at all incredible that they may some day be revived in full force. In the year 1857, at the summer assizes[20] of the county of Cornwall, an unfortunate man,* said to be of unexceptionable conduct in all relations of life, was sentenced to twenty-one months' imprisonment for uttering, and writing on a gate, some offensive words concerning Christianity. Within a month of the same time, at the Old Bailey,[21] two persons, on two separate occasions,† were rejected as jurymen, and one of them grossly insulted by the judge and one of the counsel, because they honestly declared that they had no theological belief; and a third, a foreigner,‡ for the same reason, was denied justice against a thief. This refusal of redress took place in virtue of the legal doctrine that no person can be allowed to give evidence in a court of justice who does not profess belief in a God (any god is sufficient) and in a future state, which is equivalent to declaring such persons to be outlaws, excluded from the protection of the tribunals; who may not only be robbed or assaulted with impunity, if no one but them-

---

* Thomas Pooley, Bodmin Assizes, July 31, 1857. In December following, he received a free pardon from the Crown.
† George Jacob Holyoake, August 17, 1857; Edward Truelove, July, 1857.
‡ Baron de Gleichen, Marlborough-street Police Court, August 4, 1857.

selves, or persons of similar opinions, is present, but anyone else may be robbed or assaulted with impunity if the proof of the fact depends on their evidence. The assumption on which this is grounded is that the oath is worthless of a person who does not believe in a future state—a proposition which betokens much ignorance of history in those who assent to it (since it is historically true that a large proportion of infidels in all ages have been persons of distinguished integrity and honor), and would be maintained by no one who had the smallest conception how many of the persons in greatest repute with the world, both for virtues and for attainments, are well known, at least to their intimates, to be unbelievers. The rule, besides, is suicidal and cuts away its own foundation. Under pretence that atheists must be liars, it admits the testimony of all atheists who are willing to lie, and rejects only those who brave the obloquy[22] of publicly confessing a detested creed rather than affirm a falsehood. A rule thus self-convicted of absurdity so far as regards its professed purpose can be kept in force only as a badge of hatred, a relic of persecution—a persecution, too, having the peculiarity that the qualification for undergoing it is the being clearly proved not to deserve it. The rule, and the theory it implies, are hardly less insulting to believers than to infidels. For if he who does not believe in a future state necessarily lies, it follows that they who do believe are only prevented from lying, if they are prevented, by the fear of hell. We will not do the authors and abettors of the rule the injury of supposing that the conception which they have formed of Christian virtue is drawn from their own consciousness.

These, indeed, are but rags and remnants of persecution, and may be thought to be not so much an indication of the wish to persecute, as an example of that very frequent infirmity of English minds, which makes them take a preposterous pleasure in the assertion of a bad principle, when they are no longer bad enough to desire to carry it really into practice. But unhappily there is no security in the state of the public mind that the suspension of worse forms of legal persecution, which has lasted for about the space of a generation, will continue. In this age the quiet surface of routine is as often ruffled by attempts to resuscitate past evils as to introduce new benefits. What is boasted of at the present time as the revival of religion is always, in narrow and uncultivated minds, at least as much the revival of bigotry; and where there is the strongest permanent leaven of intolerance in the feelings of a people, which at all times abides in the middle classes of this country, it needs but little to provoke them into actively persecuting those whom they

have never ceased to think proper objects of persecution.* For it is
this—it is the opinions men entertain, and the feelings they cherish,
respecting those who disown the beliefs they deem important which
makes this country not a place of mental freedom. For a long time past,
the chief mischief of the legal penalties is that they strengthen the social
stigma. It is that stigma which is really effective, and so effective is it
that the profession of opinions which are under the ban of society is
much less common in England than is, in many other countries, the
avowal of those which incur risk of judicial punishment. In respect to
all persons but those whose pecuniary[23] circumstances make them
independent of the good will of other people, opinion, on this subject,
is as efficacious as law; men might as well be imprisoned as excluded
from the means of earning their bread. Those whose bread is already
secured, and who desire no favors from men in power, or from bodies
of men, or from the public, have nothing to fear from the open avowal
of any opinions but to be ill-thought of and ill-spoken of, and this it
ought not to require a very heroic mold to enable them to bear. There is
no room for any appeal *ad misericordiam*[24] in behalf of such persons.
But though we do not now inflict so much evil on those who think differently from us as it was formerly our custom to do, it may be that we

---

* Ample warning may be drawn from the large infusion of the passions of a persecutor,
which mingled with the general display of the worst parts of our national character on the
occasion of the Sepoy Insurrection. [Editor: The Sepoy Insurrection, or Indian Mutiny,
(1857-58) was a widespread but unsuccessful rebellion against British rule in India initiated
by Indian soldiers (sepoys) in the service of the British East India Company. As a result of
the rebellion, the administration of India was transferred from the East India Company to
the Crown.] The ravings of fanatics or charlatans from the pulpit may be unworthy of
notice, but the heads of the Evangelical party have announced as their principle for the government of Hindus and Mohammedans that no schools be supported by public money in
which the Bible is not taught, and by necessary consequence that no public employment be
given to any but real or pretended Christians. An Under-Secretary of State [Editor: W.N.
Massey], in a speech delivered to his constituents on the 12th of November, 1857, is
reported to have said: "Toleration of their faith" (the faith of a hundred millions of British
subjects), "the superstition which they called religion, by the British Government, had had
the effect of retarding the ascendancy of the British name, and preventing the salutary
growth of Christianity....Toleration was the great corner-stone of the religious liberties of
this country; but do not let them abuse that precious word 'toleration.' As he understood it,
it meant the complete liberty to all, freedom of worship, *among Christians, who worshipped upon the same foundation.* It meant toleration of all sects and denominations of
Christians who believed in the one mediation." I desire to call attention to the fact that a
man who has been deemed fit to fill a high office in the government of this country, under a
liberal Ministry, maintains the doctrine that all who do not believe in the divinity of Christ
are beyond the pale of toleration. Who, after this imbecile display, can indulge the illusion
that religious persecution has passed away, never to return?

do ourselves as much evil as ever by our treatment of them. Socrates was put to death, but the Socratic philosophy rose like the sun in heaven and spread its illumination over the whole intellectual firmament. Christians were cast to the lions, but the Christian Church grew up a stately and spreading tree, overtopping the older and less vigorous growths and stifling them by its shade. Our merely social intolerance kills no one, roots out no opinions, but induces men to disguise them, or to abstain from any active effort for their diffusion. With us, heretical opinions do not perceptibly gain, or even lose, ground in each decade or generation; they never blaze out far and wide, but continue to smolder in the narrow circles of thinking and studious persons among whom they originate, without ever lighting up the general affairs of mankind with either a true or a deceptive light. And thus is kept up a state of things very satisfactory to some minds, because, without the unpleasant process of fining or imprisoning anybody, it maintains all prevailing opinions outwardly undisturbed, while it does not absolutely interdict the exercise of reason by dissentients afflicted with the malady of thought. A convenient plan for having peace in the intellectual world, and keeping all things going on therein very much as they do already. But the price paid for this sort of intellectual pacification is the sacrifice of the entire moral courage of the human mind. A state of things in which a large portion of the most active and inquiring intellects find it advisable to keep the general* principles and grounds of their convictions within their own breasts, and attempt, in what they address to the public, to fit as much as they can of their own conclusions to premises which they have internally renounced, cannot send forth the open, fearless characters and logical, consistent intellects who once adorned the thinking world. The sort of men who can be looked for under it are either mere conformers to commonplace, or time-servers for truth, whose arguments on all great subjects are meant for their hearers, and are not those which have convinced themselves. Those who avoid this alternative do so by narrowing their thoughts and interests to things which can be spoken of without venturing within the region of principles—that is, to small practical matters which would come right of themselves if but the minds of mankind were strengthened and enlarged, and which will never be made effectually right until then—while that which would strengthen and enlarge

---

* general—genuine (1859a, 1859b).

men's minds, free and daring speculation on the highest subjects, is
abandoned.

Those in whose eyes this reticence on the part of heretics is no evil
should consider, in the first place, that in consequence of it there is never
any fair and thorough discussion of heretical opinions; and that such of
them as could not stand such a discussion, though they may be prevented
from spreading, do not disappear. But it is not the minds of heretics that
are deteriorated most by the ban placed on all inquiry which does not
end in the orthodox conclusions. The greatest harm done is to those who
are not heretics, and whose whole mental development is cramped, and
their reason cowed, by the fear of heresy. Who can compute what the
world loses in the multitude of promising intellects combined with timid
characters, who dare not follow out any bold, vigorous, independent
train of thought, lest it should land them in something which would
admit of being considered irreligious or immoral? Among them we may
occasionally see some man of deep conscientiousness and subtle and
refined understanding, who spends a life in sophisticating with an intellect which he cannot silence, and exhausts the resources of ingenuity in
attempting to reconcile the promptings of his conscience and reason with
orthodoxy, which yet he does not, perhaps, to the end succeed in doing.
No one can be a great thinker who does not recognize that as a thinker it
is his first duty to follow his intellect to whatever conclusions it may
lead. Truth gains more even by the errors of one who, with due study and
preparation, thinks for himself than by the true opinions of those who
only hold them because they do not suffer themselves to think. Not that
it is solely, or chiefly, to form great thinkers that freedom of thinking is
required. On the contrary, it is as much, and even more indispensable, to
enable average human beings to attain the mental stature which they are
capable of. There have been, and may again be, great individual thinkers
in a general atmosphere of mental slavery. But there never has been, nor
ever will be, in that atmosphere, an intellectually active people. When*
any people has made a temporary approach to such a character, it has
been because the dread of heterodox speculation was for a time suspended. Where there is a tacit convention that principles are not to be
disputed, where the discussion of the greatest questions which can
occupy humanity is considered to be closed, we cannot hope to find that
generally high scale of mental activity which has made some periods of

---

* When—Where (1859a, 19859b).

history so remarkable. Never when controversy avoided the subjects which are large and important enough to kindle enthusiasm was the mind of a people stirred up from its foundations, and the impulse given which raised even persons of the most ordinary intellect to something of the dignity of thinking beings. Of such we have had an example in the condition of Europe during the times immediately following the Reformation; another, though limited to the Continent and to a more cultivated class, in the speculative movement of the latter-half of the eighteenth century; and a third, of still briefer duration, in the intellectual fermentation of Germany during the Goethian and Fichtean period.[25] These periods differed widely in the particular opinions which they developed, but were alike in this: that during all three the yoke of authority was broken. In each, an old mental despotism had been thrown off, and no new one had yet taken its place. The impulse given at these three periods has made Europe what it now is. Every single improvement which has taken place either in the human mind or in institutions may be traced distinctly to one or other of them. Appearances have for some time indicated that all three impulses are well near spent; and we can expect no fresh start until we again assert our mental freedom.

Let us now pass to the second division of the argument, and dismissing the supposition that any of the received opinions may be false, let us assume them to be true and examine into the worth of the manner in which they are likely to be held when their truth is not freely and openly canvassed. However unwillingly a person who has a strong opinion may admit the possibility that his opinion may be false, he ought to be moved by the consideration that however true it may be, if it is not fully, frequently, and fearlessly discussed, it will be held as a dead dogma, not a living truth.

There is a class of persons (happily not quite so numerous as formerly) who think it enough if a person assents undoubtingly to what they think true, though he has no knowledge whatever of the grounds of the opinion and could not make a tenable defense of it against the most superficial objections. Such persons, if they can once get their creed taught from authority, naturally think that no good, and some harm, comes of its being allowed to be questioned. Where their influence prevails, they make it nearly impossible for the received opinion to be rejected wisely and considerately, though it may still be rejected rashly and ignorantly; for to shut out discussion entirely is seldom possible, and when it once gets in, beliefs not grounded on conviction are apt to give way before the

dead dogma

slightest semblance of an argument. Waiving, however, this possibility—assuming that the true opinion abides in the mind, but abides as a prejudice, a belief independent of, and proof against, argument—this is not the way in which truth ought to be held by a rational being. This is not knowing the truth. Truth, thus held, is but one superstition the more, accidentally clinging to the words which enunciate a truth.

If the intellect and judgment of mankind ought to be cultivated, a thing which Protestants at least do not deny, on what can these faculties be more appropriately exercised by anyone than on the things which concern him so much that it is considered necessary for him to hold opinions on them? If the cultivation of the understanding consists in one thing more than in another, it is surely in learning the grounds of one's own opinions. Whatever people believe, on subjects on which it is of the first importance to believe rightly, they ought to be able to defend against at least the common objections. But, someone may say, "Let them be *taught* the grounds of their opinions. It does not follow that opinions must be merely parroted because they are never heard controverted. Persons who learn geometry do not simply commit the theorems to memory, but understand and learn likewise the demonstrations; and it would be absurd to say that they remain ignorant of the grounds of geometrical truths because they never hear anyone deny and attempt to disprove them." Undoubtedly: and such teaching suffices on a subject like mathematics, where there is nothing at all to be said on the wrong side of the question. The peculiarity of the evidence of mathematical truths is that all the argument is on one side. There are no objections, and no answers to objections. But on every subject on which difference of opinion is possible, the truth depends on a balance to be struck between two sets of conflicting reasons. Even in natural philosophy, there is always some other explanation possible of the same facts—some geocentric theory instead of heliocentric, some phlogiston instead of oxygen—and it has to be shown why that other theory cannot be the true one;[26] and until this is shown and until we know how it is shown, we do not understand the grounds of our opinion. But when we turn to subjects infinitely more complicated—to morals, religion, politics, social relations, and the business of life—three-fourths of the arguments for every disputed opinion consist in dispelling the appearances which favor some opinion different from it. The greatest orator, save one, of antiquity,[27] has left it on record that he always studied his adversary's case with as great, if not with still greater, intensity than even his own. What Cicero practiced as the means of forensic success requires to be imitated by all who study any subject in order to arrive at the truth. He who knows only his own side of the case knows little of that. His reasons may be good, and no one may have been able to refute them. But if he is equally unable to refute the reasons on the opposite side, if he does not so much as know what they are, he has no ground for preferring either opinion. The rational position for him would be suspension of judgment, and unless he contents himself with that, he is either led by authority or adopts, like the generality of the world, the side to which he feels most inclination. Nor is it enough that he should hear the arguments of adversaries from his own teachers, presented as they state them, and accompanied by what they offer as refutations. This is not the way to do justice to the arguments or bring them into real contact with his own mind. He must be able to hear them from persons who actually believe them, who defend them in earnest and do their very utmost for them. He must know them in their most plausible and persuasive form; he must feel the whole force of the difficulty which the true view of the subject has to encounter and dispose of, [or] else he will never really possess himself of the portion of truth which meets and removes that difficulty. Ninety-nine in a hundred of what are called educated men are in this condition, even of those who can argue fluently for their opinions. Their conclusion may be true, but it might be false for anything they know; they have never thrown themselves into the mental position of those who think differently from them and considered what such persons may have to say; and, consequently, they do not, in any proper sense of the word, know the doctrine which they themselves profess. They do not know those parts of it which explain and justify the remainder—the considerations which show that a fact which seemingly conflicts with another is reconcilable with it, or that, of two apparently strong reasons, one and not the other ought to be preferred. All that part of the truth which turns the scale and decides the judgment of a completely informed mind, they are strangers to; nor is it ever really known but to those who have attended equally and impartially to both sides and endeavored to see the reasons of both in the strongest light. So essential is this discipline to a real understanding of moral and human subjects that, if opponents of all important truths do not exist, it is indispensable to imagine them and supply them with the strongest arguments which the most skillful devil's advocate can conjure up.

To abate the force of these considerations, an enemy of free discussion may be supposed to say that there is no necessity for mankind in general to know and understand all that can be said against or for their opinions by philosophers and theologians. That it is not needful for common men to be able to expose all the misstatements or fallacies of an ingenious opponent. That it is enough if there is always somebody capable of answering them, so that nothing likely to mislead uninstructed persons remains unrefuted. That simple minds, having been taught the obvious grounds of the truths inculcated on them, may trust to authority for the rest and, being aware that they have neither knowledge nor talent to resolve every difficulty which can be raised, may repose in the assurance that all those which have been raised have been or can be answered by those who are specially trained to the task.

Conceding to this view of the subject the utmost that can be claimed for it by those most easily satisfied with the amount of understanding of truth which ought to accompany the belief of it, even so, the argument for free discussion is no way weakened. For even this doctrine acknowledges that mankind ought to have a rational assurance that all objections have been satisfactorily answered; and how are they to be answered if that which requires to be answered is not spoken? Or how can the answer be known to be satisfactory if the objectors have no opportunity of showing that it is unsatisfactory? If not the public, at least the philosophers and theologians who are to resolve the difficulties must make themselves familiar with those difficulties in their most puzzling form; and this cannot be accomplished unless they are freely stated and placed in the most advantageous light which they admit of. The Catholic Church has its own way of dealing with this embarrassing problem. It makes a broad separation between those who can be permitted to receive its doctrines on conviction, and those who must accept them on trust. Neither, indeed, are allowed any choice as to what they will accept; but the clergy, such at least as can be fully confided in, may admissibly and meritoriously make themselves acquainted with the arguments of opponents in order to answer them, and may, therefore, read heretical books; the laity, not unless by special permission, hard to be obtained. This discipline recognizes a knowledge of the enemy's case as beneficial to the teachers, but finds means, consistent with this, of denying it to the rest of the world, thus giving to the *élite* more mental culture, though not more mental freedom, than it allows to the mass. By this device it succeeds in obtaining the kind of mental superiority which its purposes require; for though culture without freedom never made a large and liberal mind, it can make a clever *nisi prius*[28] advocate of a cause. But in countries professing Protestantism, this resource is denied, since Protestants hold, at least in theory, that the responsibility for the choice of a religion must be borne by each for himself and cannot be thrown off upon teachers.

Besides, in the present state of the world, it is practically impossible that writings which are read by the instructed can be kept from the uninstructed. If the teachers of mankind are to be cognizant of all that they ought to know, everything must be free to be written and published without restraint.

If, however, the mischievous operation of the absence of free discussion, when the received opinions are true, were confined to leaving men ignorant of the grounds of those opinions, it might be thought that this, if an intellectual, is no moral evil and does not affect the worth of the opinions regarded in their influence on the character. The fact, however, is that not only the grounds of the opinion are forgotten in the absence of discussion, but too often the meaning of the opinion itself. The words which convey it cease to suggest ideas, or suggest only a small portion of those they were originally employed to communicate. Instead of a vivid conception and a living belief, there remain only a few phrases retained by rote; or, if any part, the shell and husk only of the meaning is retained, the finer essence being lost. The great chapter in human history which this fact occupies and fills cannot be too earnestly studied and meditated on.

It is illustrated in the experience of almost all ethical doctrines and religious creeds. They are all full of meaning and vitality to those who originate them, and to the direct disciples of the originators. Their meaning continues to be felt in undiminished strength, and is perhaps brought out into even fuller consciousness, so long as the struggle lasts to give the doctrine or creed an ascendancy over other creeds. At last it either prevails and becomes the general opinion, or its progress stops; it keeps possession of the ground it has gained, but ceases to spread further. When either of these results has become apparent, controversy on the subject flags, and gradually dies away. The doctrine has taken its place, if not as a received opinion, as one of the admitted sects or divisions of opinion; those who hold it have generally inherited, not adopted it; and conversion from one of these doctrines to another, being now an exceptional fact, occupies little place in the thoughts of their professors. Instead of being, as at first, constantly on the alert either to defend themselves against the world or to bring the world over to them, they have subsided into acquiescence, and neither listen, when they can help it, to arguments against their creed, nor trouble dissentients (if there are such) with arguments in its favor. From this time may usually be dated the decline in the living power of the doctrine. We often hear the teachers of all creeds lamenting the difficulty of keeping up in the minds of believers a lively apprehension of the truth which they nominally recognize, so that it may penetrate the feelings and acquire a real mastery over the conduct. No such difficulty is complained of while the creed is still fighting for its existence; even the weaker combatants then know and feel what they are fighting for, and the difference between it and other doctrines; and, in that period of every creed's existence, not a few persons may be found who have realized its fundamental principles in all the forms of thought, have weighed and considered them in all their important bearings, and have experienced the full effect on the character which belief in that creed ought to produce in a mind thoroughly imbued with it. But when it has come to be a hereditary creed, and to be received passively, not actively—when the mind is no longer compelled, in the same degree as at first, to exercise its vital powers on the questions which its belief presents to it—there is a progressive tendency to forget all of the belief except the formularies,[29] or to give it a dull and torpid assent, as if accepting it on trust dispensed with the necessity of realizing it in consciousness, or testing it by personal experience, until it almost ceases to connect itself at all with the inner life of the human being. Then are seen the cases, so frequent in this age of the world as almost to form the majority, in which the creed remains as it were outside the mind, encrusting and petrifying it against all other influences addressed to the higher parts of our nature; manifesting its power by not suffering any fresh and living conviction to get in, but itself doing nothing for the mind or heart, except standing sentinel over them to keep them vacant.

To what an extent doctrines intrinsically fitted to make the deepest impression upon the mind may remain in it as dead beliefs, without being ever realized in the imagination, the feelings, or the understanding, is exemplified by the manner in which the majority of believers hold the doctrines of Christianity. By *Christianity* I here mean what is accounted such by all churches and sects—the maxims and precepts contained in the New Testament. These are considered sacred and accepted as laws by all professing Christians. Yet it is scarcely too much to say that not one Christian in a thousand guides or tests his individual conduct by reference to those laws. The standard to which he does refer it is the custom of his nation, his class, or his religious profession. He has thus, on the one hand, a collection of ethical maxims which he believes to have been vouchsafed to him by infallible wisdom as rules for his government; and, on the other, a set of everyday judgments and practices which go a certain length with some of those maxims, not so great a length with others, stand in direct opposition to some, and are, on the whole, a compromise between the Christian creed and the interests and suggestions of worldly life. To the first of these standards he gives his homage; to the other his real allegiance. All Christians believe that the blessed are the poor and humble, and those who are ill-used by the world; that it is easier for a camel to pass through the eye of a needle than for a rich man to enter the kingdom of heaven; that they should judge not, lest they be judged; that they should swear not at all; that they should love their neighbor as themselves; that if one take their cloak, they should give him their coat also; that they should take no thought for tomorrow; that if they would be perfect, they should sell all that they have and give it to the poor.[30] They are not insincere when they say that they believe these things. They do believe them, as people believe what they have always heard lauded and never discussed. But in the sense of that living belief which regulates conduct, they believe these doctrines just up to the point to which it is usual to act upon them. The doctrines in their integrity are serviceable to pelt adversaries with; and it is understood that they are to be put forward (when possible) as the reasons for whatever people do that they think laudable. But anyone who reminded them that the maxims require an infinity of things which they never even think of doing, would gain nothing but to be classed among those very unpopular characters who affect to be better than other people. The doctrines have no hold on ordinary believers—are not a power in their minds. They have a habitual respect for the sound of them, but no feeling which spreads from the words to the things signified and forces the mind to take *them* in and make them conform to the formula. Whenever conduct is concerned, they look round for Mr. A and B to direct them how far to go in obeying Christ.

Now we may be well assured that the case was not thus, but far otherwise, with the early Christians. Had it been thus, Christianity never would have expanded from an obscure sect of the despised Hebrews into the religion of the Roman Empire. When their enemies said, "See how these Christians love one another"[31] (a remark not likely to be made by anybody now), they assuredly had a much livelier feeling of the meaning of their creed than they have ever had since. And to this cause, probably, it is chiefly owing that Christianity now makes so little progress in extending its domain, and after eighteen centuries is still nearly confined to Europeans and the descendants of Europeans. Even with the strictly religious, who are much in earnest about their doctrines and attach a greater amount of meaning to many of them than people in general, it commonly happens that the part which is thus comparatively active in their minds is that which was made by Calvin, or Knox,[32] or some such person much nearer in character to themselves. The sayings of Christ coexist passively in their minds, producing hardly any effect beyond what is caused by mere listening to words so amiable and bland. There are many reasons, doubtless, why doctrines which are the badge of a sect retain more of their vitality than those common to all recognized sects, and why more pains are taken by teachers to keep their meaning alive; but one reason certainly is that the peculiar doctrines are more questioned and have to be more often defended against open gainsayers. Both teachers and learners go to sleep at their post as soon as there is no enemy in the field.

The same thing holds true, generally speaking, of all traditional doctrines—those of prudence and knowledge of life, as well as of morals or religion. All languages and literatures are full of general observations on life, both as to what it is and how to conduct oneself in it—observations which everybody knows, which everybody repeats or hears with acquiescence, which are received as truisms, yet of which most people first truly learn the meaning when experience, generally of a painful kind, has made it a reality to them. How often, when smarting under some unforeseen misfortune or disappointment, does a person call to mind some proverb or common saying, familiar to him all his life, the meaning of which, if he had ever before felt it as he does now, would have saved him from the calamity. There are indeed reasons for this other than the absence of discussion: there are many truths of which the full meaning *cannot* be realized until personal experience has brought it home. But much more of the meaning even of these would have been understood, and what was understood would have been far more deeply impressed on the mind, if the man had been accustomed to hear it argued *pro* and *con* by people who did understand it. The fatal tendency of mankind to leave off thinking about a thing when it is no longer doubtful is the cause of half their errors. A contemporary author has well spoken of "the deep slumber of a decided opinion."[33]

But what?! (It may be asked.) Is the absence of unanimity an indispensable condition of true knowledge? Is it necessary that some part of mankind should persist in error to enable any to realize the truth? Does a belief cease to be real and vital as soon as it is generally received—and is a proposition never thoroughly understood and felt unless some doubt of it remains? As soon as mankind have unanimously accepted a truth, does the truth perish within them? The highest aim and best result of improved intelligence, it has till now been thought, is to unite mankind more and more in the acknowledgment of all important truths—and does the intelligence only last as long as it has not achieved its object? Do the fruits of conquest perish by the very completeness of the victory?

I affirm no such thing. As mankind improve, the number of doctrines which are no longer disputed or doubted will be constantly on the increase; and the well-being of mankind may almost be measured by the number and gravity of the truths which have reached the point of being uncontested. The cessation, on one question after another, of serious controversy is one of the necessary incidents of the consolidation of opinion—a consolidation as salutary in the case of true opinions as it is dangerous and noxious when the opinions are erroneous. But though this gradual narrowing of the bounds of diversity of opinion is necessary in both senses of the term, being at once inevitable and indispensable, we are not therefore obliged to conclude that all its consequences must be beneficial. The loss of so important an aid to the intelligent and living apprehension of a truth as is afforded by the necessity of explaining it to, or defending it against, opponents, though not sufficient to outweigh, is no trifling drawback from the benefit of its universal recognition. Where this advantage can no longer be had, I confess I should like to see the teachers of mankind endeavoring to provide a substitute for it—some contrivance for making the difficulties of the question as present to the learner's consciousness as if they were pressed upon him by a dissentient champion eager for his conversion.

But instead of seeking contrivances for this purpose, they have lost those they formerly had. The Socratic dialectics, so magnificently exemplified in the dialogues of Plato, were a contrivance of this description. They were essentially a negative discussion of the great questions of philosophy and life, directed with consummate skill to the purpose of convincing anyone who had merely adopted the commonplaces of received opinion that he did not understand the subject—that he as yet attached no definite meaning to the doctrines he professed; in order that, becoming aware of his ignorance, he might be put in the way to attain a stable belief resting on a clear apprehension both of the meaning of doctrines and of their evidence. The school disputations of the Middle Ages had a somewhat similar object.[34] They were intended to make sure that the pupil understood his own opinion, and (by necessary correlation) the opinion opposed to it, and could enforce the grounds of the one and confute those of the other. These last-mentioned contests had indeed the incurable defect that the premises appealed to were taken from authority, not from reason; and, as a discipline to the mind, they were in every respect inferior to the powerful dialectics which formed the intellects of the "*Socratici viri;*"[35] but the modern mind owes far more to both than it is generally willing to admit, and the present modes of education contain nothing which in the smallest degree supplies the place either of the one or of the other. A person who derives all his instruction from teachers or books, even if he escape the besetting temptation of contenting himself with cram, is under no compulsion to hear both sides; accordingly it is far from a frequent accomplishment, even among thinkers, to know both sides; and the weakest part of what everybody says in defense of his opinion is what he intends as a reply to antagonists. It is the fashion of the present time to disparage negative logic—that which points out weaknesses in theory or errors in practice without establishing positive truths. Such negative criticism would indeed be poor enough as an ultimate result, but as a means to attaining any positive knowledge or conviction worthy the name it cannot be valued too highly; and until people are again systematically trained to it, there will be few great thinkers, and a low general average of intellect in any but the mathematical and physical departments of speculation. On any other subject no one's opinions deserve the name of knowledge, except so far as he has either had forced upon him by others, or gone through of himself, the same mental process which would have been required of him in carrying on an active controversy with opponents. That, therefore, which, when absent, it is so indispensable, but so difficult, to create, how worse than absurd it is* to forego when spontaneously offering itself! If there are any persons who contest a received opinion, or who will do so if law or opinion will let them, let us thank them for it, open our minds to listen to them, and rejoice that there is someone to do for us what we otherwise ought, if we have any regard for either the certainty or the vitality of our convictions, to do with much greater labor for ourselves.

It still remains to speak of one of the principal causes which make diversity of opinion advantageous, and will continue to do so until mankind shall have entered a stage of intellectual advancement which at present seems at an incalculable distance. We have hitherto considered only two possibilities: that the received opinion may be false, and some other opinion, consequently, true; or that, the received opinion being true, a conflict with the opposite error is essential to a clear apprehension and deep feeling of its truth. But there is a commoner case than either of these: when the conflicting doctrines, instead of being one true and the

---

* it is—is it (1859a, 1859b).

other false, share the truth between them, and the nonconforming opinion is needed to supply the remainder of the truth of which the received doctrine embodies only a part. Popular opinions, on subjects not palpable to sense, are often true, but seldom or never the whole truth. They are a part of the truth—sometimes a greater, sometimes a smaller part, but exaggerated, distorted, and disjoined from the truths by which they ought to be accompanied and limited. Heretical opinions, on the other hand, are generally some of these suppressed and neglected truths, bursting the bonds which kept them down, and either seeking reconciliation with the truth contained in the common opinion, or fronting[36] it as enemies, and setting themselves up, with similar exclusiveness, as the whole truth. The latter case is hitherto the most frequent, as, in the human mind, one-sidedness has always been the rule, and many-sidedness the exception. Hence, even in revolutions of opinion, one part of the truth usually sets while another rises. Even progress, which ought to superadd, for the most part only substitutes one partial and incomplete truth for another; improvement consisting chiefly in this, that the new fragment of truth is more wanted, more adapted to the needs of the time than that which it displaces. Such being the partial character of prevailing opinions, even when resting on a true foundation, every opinion which embodies something of the portion of truth which the common opinion omits ought to be considered precious, with whatever amount of error and confusion that truth may be blended. No sober judge of human affairs will feel bound to be indignant because those who force on our notice truths which we should otherwise have overlooked, overlook some of those which we see. Rather, he will think that so long as popular truth is one-sided, it is more desirable than otherwise that unpopular truth should have one-sided asserters too, such being usually the most energetic and the most likely to compel reluctant attention to the fragment of wisdom which they proclaim as if it were the whole.

Thus, in the eighteenth century, when nearly all the instructed, and all those of the uninstructed who were led by them, were lost in admiration of what is called civilization and of the marvels of modern science, literature, and philosophy, and while greatly overrating the amount of unlikeness between the men of modern and those of ancient times, indulged the belief that the whole of the difference was in their own favor; with what a salutary shock did the paradoxes of Rousseau[37] explode like bombshells in the midst, dislocating the compact mass of one-sided opinion and forcing its elements to recombine in a better form and with additional ingredients. Not that the current opinions were on the whole farther from the truth than Rousseau's were; on the contrary, they were nearer to it; they contained more of positive truth, and very much less of error. Nevertheless there lay in Rousseau's doctrine, and has floated down the stream of opinion along with it, a considerable amount of exactly those truths which the popular opinion wanted; and these are the deposit which was left behind when the flood subsided. The superior worth of simplicity of life, the enervating[38] and demoralizing effect of the trammels[39] and hypocrisies of artificial society are ideas which have never been entirely absent from cultivated minds since Rousseau wrote; and they will in time produce their due effect, though at present needing to be asserted as much as ever, and to be asserted by deeds, for words, on this subject, have nearly exhausted their power.

In politics, again, it is almost a commonplace that a party of order or stability and a party of progress or reform are both necessary elements of a healthy state of political life, until the one or the other shall have so enlarged its mental grasp as to be a party equally of order and of progress, knowing and distinguishing what is fit to be preserved from what ought to be swept away. Each of these modes of thinking derives its utility from the deficiencies of the other; but it is in a great measure the opposition of the other that keeps each within the limits of reason and sanity. Unless opinions favorable to democracy and to aristocracy, to property and to equality, to co-operation and to competition, to luxury and to abstinence, to sociality and individuality, to liberty and discipline, and all the other standing antagonisms of practical life, are expressed with equal freedom and enforced and defended with equal talent and energy, there is no chance of both elements obtaining their due; one scale is sure to go up, and the other down. Truth, in the great practical concerns of life, is so much a question of the reconciling and combining of opposites that very few have minds sufficiently capacious and impartial to make the adjustment with an approach to correctness, and it has to be made by the rough process of a struggle between combatants fighting under hostile banners. On any of the great open questions just enumerated, if either of the two opinions has a better claim than the other, not merely to be tolerated, but to be encouraged and countenanced, it is the one which happens at the particular time and place to be in a minority. That is the opinion which, for the time being, represents the neglected interests, the side of human well-being which is in danger of obtaining less than its share. I am aware that there is not, in this country, any intolerance of differences of opinion on most of these topics. They are adduced to show, by admitted and multiplied examples, the universality of the fact that only through diversity of opinion is there, in the existing state of human intellect, a chance of fair play to all sides of the truth. When there are persons to be found who form an exception to the apparent unanimity of the world on any subject, even if the world is in the right, it is always probable that dissentients have something worth hearing to say for themselves, and that truth would lose something by their silence.

It may be objected, "But *some* received principles, especially on the highest and most vital subjects, are more than half-truths. The Christian morality, for instance, is the whole truth on that subject, and if anyone teaches a morality which varies from it, he is wholly in error." As this is of all cases the most important in practice, none can be fitter to test the general maxim. But before pronouncing what Christian morality is or is not, it would be desirable to decide what is meant by *Christian morality*. If it means the morality of the New Testament, I wonder that anyone who derives his knowledge of this from the book itself can suppose that it was announced, or intended, as a complete doctrine of morals. The Gospel always refers to a preexisting morality and confines its precepts to the particulars in which that morality was to be corrected or superseded by a wider and higher, expressing itself, moreover, in terms most general, often impossible to be interpreted literally, and possessing rather the impressiveness of poetry or eloquence than the precision of legislation. To extract from it a body of ethical doctrine has never been possible without eking it out from the Old Testament, that is, from a system elaborate indeed, but in many respects barbarous and intended only for a barbarous people. St. Paul, a declared enemy to this Judaic mode of interpreting the doctrine and filling up the scheme of his Master, equally assumes a preexisting morality, namely, that of the Greeks and Romans; and his advice to Christians is in a great measure a system of accommodation to that, even to the extent of giving an apparent sanction to slavery.[40] What is called *Christian*, but should rather be termed *theological*, morality was not the work of Christ or the Apostles, but is of much later origin, having been gradually built up by the Catholic church of the first five centuries, and though not implicitly adopted by moderns and Protestants, has been much less modified by them than might have been expected. For the most part, indeed, they have contented themselves with cutting off the additions which had been made to it in the Middle Ages, each sect supplying the place by fresh additions, adapted to its own character and tendencies. That mankind owe a great debt to this morality, and to its early teachers, I should be the last person to deny; but I do not scruple to say of it that it is, in many important points, incomplete and one-sided, and that unless ideas and feelings not sanctioned by it had contributed to the formation of European life and character, human affairs would have been in a worse condition than they now are. Christian morality (so called) has all the characters of a reaction; it is, in great part, a protest against paganism. Its ideal is negative rather than positive; passive rather than active; innocence rather than nobleness; abstinence from evil, rather than energetic pursuit of good; in its precepts (as has been well said) "thou shalt not" predominates unduly over "thou shalt." In its horror of sensuality, it made an idol of asceticism, which has been gradually compromised away into one of legality. It holds out the hope of heaven and the threat of hell as the appointed and appropriate motives to a virtuous life—in this falling far below the best of the ancients, and doing what lies in it to give to human morality an essentially selfish character by disconnecting each man's feelings of duty from the interests of his fellow creatures, except so far as a self-interested inducement is offered to him for consulting them. It is essentially a doctrine of passive obedience; it inculcates submission to all authorities found established; who indeed are not to be actively obeyed when they command what religion forbids, but who are not to be resisted, far less rebelled against, for any amount of wrong to ourselves. And while, in the morality of the best pagan nations, duty to the state holds even a disproportionate place, infringing on the just liberty of the individual, in purely Christian ethics that grand department of duty is scarcely noticed or acknowledged. It is in the Koran, not the New Testament, that we read the maxim, "A ruler who appoints any man to an office, when there is in his dominions another man better qualified for it, sins against God and against the state."[41] What little recognition the idea of obligation to the public obtains in modern morality is derived from Greek and Roman sources, not from Christian; as, even in the morality of private life, whatever exists of magnanimity, high-mindedness, personal dignity, even the sense of honor, is derived from the purely human, not the religious part of our education, and never could have grown out of a standard of ethics in which the only worth professedly recognized is that of obedience.

I am as far as anyone from pretending that these defects are necessarily inherent in the Christian ethics in every manner in which it can be conceived, or that the many requisites of a complete moral doctrine which it does not contain do not admit of being reconciled with it. Far less would I insinuate this of the doctrines and precepts of Christ himself. I believe that the sayings of Christ are all that I can see any evidence of their having been intended to be; that they are irreconcilable with nothing which a comprehensive morality requires; that everything which is excellent in ethics may be brought within them, with no greater violence to their language than has been done to it by all who have attempted to deduce from them any practical system of conduct whatever. But it is quite consistent with this to believe that they contain, and were meant to contain, only a part of the truth; that many essential elements of the highest morality are among the things which are not provided for, nor intended to be provided for, in the recorded deliverances of the Founder of Christianity, and which have been entirely thrown aside in the system of ethics erected on the basis of those deliverances by the Christian Church. And this being so, I think it a great error to persist in attempting to find in the Christian doctrine that complete rule for our guidance which its author intended it to sanction and enforce, but only partially to provide. I believe, too, that this narrow theory is becoming a grave practical evil, detracting greatly from the value of the moral training and instruction which so many well-meaning persons are now at length exerting themselves to promote. I much fear that by attempting to form the mind and feelings on an exclusively religious type, and discarding those secular standards (as for want of a better name they may be called) which formerly co-existed with and supplemented the Christian ethics, receiving some of its spirit, and infusing into it some of theirs, there will result, and is even now resulting, a low, abject, servile type of character which, submit itself as it may to what it deems the Supreme Will, is incapable of rising to or sympathizing in the conception of Supreme Goodness. I believe that other ethics than any which can be evolved from exclusively Christian sources must exist side by side with Christian ethics to produce the moral regeneration of mankind; and that the Christian system is no exception to the rule that, in an imperfect state of the human mind, the interests of truth require a diversity of opinions. It is not necessary that in ceasing to ignore the moral truths not contained in Christianity men should ignore any of those which it does contain. Such prejudice, or oversight, when it occurs, is altogether an evil, but it is one from which we cannot hope to be always exempt, and must be regarded as the price paid for an inestimable good. The exclusive pretension made by a part of the truth to be the whole must and ought to be protested against; and if a reactionary impulse should make the protestors unjust in their turn, this one-sidedness, like the other, may be lamented, but must be tolerated. If Christians would teach infidels to be just to Christianity, they should themselves be just to infidelity. It can do truth no service to blink the fact, known to all who have the most ordinary acquaintance with literary history, that a large portion of the noblest and most valuable moral teaching has been the work, not only of men who did not know, but of men who knew and rejected, the Christian faith.

I do not pretend that the most unlimited use of the freedom of enunciating all possible opinions would put an end to the evils of religious or philosophical sectarianism. Every truth which men of narrow capacity are in earnest about is sure to be asserted, inculcated, and in many ways even acted on, as if no other truth existed in the world, or at all events none that could limit or qualify the first. I acknowledge that the tendency of all opinions to become sectarian is not cured by the freest discussion, but is often heightened and exacerbated thereby; the truth which ought to have been, but was not, seen, being rejected all the more violently because proclaimed by persons regarded as opponents. But it is not on the impassioned partisan, it is on the calmer and more disinterested bystander, that this collision of opinions works its salutary effect. Not the violent conflict between parts of the truth, but the quiet suppression of half of it, is the formidable evil; there is always hope when people are forced to listen to both sides; it is when they attend only to one that errors harden into prejudices, and truth itself ceases to have the effect of truth by being exaggerated into falsehood. And since there are few mental attributes more rare than that judicial faculty which can sit in intelligent judgment between two sides of a question, of which only one is represented by an advocate before it, truth has no chance but in proportion as every side of it, every opinion which embodies any fraction of the truth, not only finds advocates, but is so advocated as to be listened to.

We have now recognized the necessity to the mental well-being of mankind (on which all their other well-being depends) of freedom of opinion, and freedom of the expression of opinion, on four distinct grounds, which we will now briefly recapitulate.

First, if any opinion is compelled to silence, that opinion may, for all we can certainly know, be true. To deny this is to assume our own infallibility.

Secondly, though the silenced opinion is an error, it may, and very commonly does, contain a portion of truth; and since the general or prevailing opinion on any object is rarely or never the whole truth, it is only by the collision of adverse opinions that the remainder of the truth has any chance of being supplied.

Thirdly, even if the received opinion is not only true, but the whole truth; unless it is suffered to be, and actually is, vigorously and earnestly contested, it will, by most of those who receive it, be held in the manner of a prejudice, with little comprehension or feeling of its rational grounds. And not only this, but, fourthly, the meaning of the doctrine itself will be in danger of being lost or enfeebled, and deprived of its vital effect on the character and conduct: the dogma becoming a mere formal profession, inefficacious for good, but encumbering the ground and preventing the growth of any real and heartfelt conviction from reason or personal experience.

Before quitting the subject of freedom of opinion, it is fit to take notice of those who say that the free expression of all opinions should be permitted on condition that the manner is temperate and does not pass the bounds of fair discussion. Much might be said on the impossibility of fixing where these supposed bounds are to be placed; for if the test is offense to those whose opinion is attacked, I think experience testifies that this offense is given whenever the attack is telling and powerful, and that every opponent who pushes them hard, and whom they find it difficult to answer, appears to them, if he shows any strong feeling on the subject, an intemperate opponent. But this, though an important consideration in a practical point of view, merges in a more fundamental objection. Undoubtedly the manner of asserting an opinion, even though it is a true one, may be very objectionable, and may justly incur severe censure. But the principal offenses of the kind are such as it is mostly impossible, unless by accidental self-betrayal, to bring home to conviction. The gravest of them is, to argue sophistically,[42] to suppress facts or arguments, to misstate the elements of the case, or misrepresent the opposite opinion. But all this, even to the most aggravated degree, is so continually done in perfect good faith by persons who are not considered, and in many other respects may not deserve to be considered, ignorant or incompetent, that it is rarely possible on adequate grounds conscientiously to stamp the misrepresentation as morally culpable, and still less could law presume to interfere with this kind of controversial misconduct. With regard to what is commonly meant by intemperate discussion—namely, invective, sarcasm, personality, and the like—the denunciation of these weapons would deserve more sympathy if it were ever proposed to interdict them equally to both sides; but it is only desired to restrain the employment of them against the prevailing opinion; against the unprevailing they may not only be used without general disapproval, but will be likely to obtain for him who uses them the praise of honest zeal and righteous indignation. Yet whatever mischief arises from their use is greatest when they are employed against the comparatively defenseless; and whatever unfair advantage can be derived by any opinion from this mode of asserting it, accrues almost exclusively to received opinions. The worst offense of this kind which can be committed by a polemic is to stigmatize those who hold the contrary opinion as bad and immoral men. To calumny[43] of this sort, those who hold any unpopular opinion are peculiarly exposed, because they are in general few and uninfluential, and nobody but themselves feels much interested* in seeing justice done them; but this weapon is, from the nature of the case, denied to those who attack a prevailing opinion: they can neither use it with safety to themselves, nor, if they could, would it do anything but recoil on their own cause. In general, opinions contrary to those commonly received can only obtain a hearing by studied moderation of language and the most cautious avoidance of unnecessary offense, from which they hardly ever deviate even in a slight degree without losing ground; while unmeasured vituperation[44] employed on the side of the prevailing opinion really does deter people from professing contrary opinions and from listening to those who profess them. For the interest, therefore, of truth and justice, it is far more important to restrain this employment of vituperative language than the other; and, for example, if it were necessary to choose, there would be much more need to discourage offensive attacks on infidelity than on religion. It is, however, obvious that law and authority have no business with restraining either, while opinion ought, in every instance, to determine its verdict by the circumstances of the individual case—condemning everyone, on whichever side of the argument he places himself, in whose mode of advocacy either want of candor, or malignity, bigotry, or intolerance of feeling manifest themselves; but not inferring these vices from the side which a person takes, though it is the contrary side of the question to our own; and giving merited honor to everyone, whatever opinion he may hold, who has calmness to see and honesty to state what his opponents and their opinions really are, exaggerating nothing to their discredit, keeping nothing back which tells, or can be supposed to tell, in their favor. This is the real morality of public discussion; and if often violated, I am happy to think that there are many controversialists who to a great extent observe it and a still greater number who conscientiously strive towards it.

---

* interested—interest (1859a, 1859b).

Be your own person
Don't be a nuisance to others
Don't harm others
Don't conform to the popular opinion

CHAPTER III

Of Individuality, As One of the Elements of Well-Being

SUCH being the reasons which make it imperative that human beings should be free to form opinions and to express their opinions without reserve; and such the baneful consequences to the intellectual, and through that to the moral nature of man, unless this liberty is either conceded or asserted in spite of prohibition; let us next examine whether the same reasons do not require that men should be free to act upon their opinions—to carry these out in their lives, without hindrance, either physical or moral, from their fellow-men, so long as it is at their own risk and peril. This last proviso is of course indispensable. No one pretends that actions should be as free as opinions. On the contrary, even opinions lose their immunity when the circumstances in which they are expressed are such as to constitute their expression a positive instigation to some mischievous act.[1] An opinion that corn-dealers are starvers of the poor, or that private property is robbery, ought to be unmolested when simply circulated through the press, but may justly incur punishment when delivered orally to an excited mob assembled before the house of a corn-dealer, or when handed about among the same mob in the form of a placard. Acts, of whatever kind, which without justifiable cause do harm to others, may be, and in the more important cases absolutely require to be, controlled by the unfavorable sentiments, and, when needful, by the active interference of mankind. The liberty of the individual must be thus far limited; he must not make himself a nuisance to other people. But if he refrains from molesting others in what concerns them, and merely acts according to his own inclination and judgment in things which concern himself, the same reasons which show that opinion should be free prove also that he should be allowed, without molestation, to carry his opinions into practice at his own cost. That mankind are not infallible; that their truths, for the most part, are only half-truths; that unity of opinion, unless resulting from the fullest and freest comparison of opposite opinions, is not desirable, and diversity not an evil, but a good, until mankind are much more capable than at present of recognizing all sides of the truth—are principles applicable to men's modes of action, not less than to their opinions. As it is useful that while mankind are imperfect there should be different opinions, so is it that there should be different experiments of living; that free scope should be given to varieties of character, short of injury to others; and that the worth of different modes of life should be proved practically, when anyone thinks fit to try them. It is desirable, in short, that in things which do not primarily concern others, individuality should assert itself. Where not the person's own character but the traditions or customs of other people are the rule of conduct, there is wanting one of the principal ingredients of human happiness, and quite the chief ingredient of individual and social progress.

In maintaining this principle, the greatest difficulty to be encountered does not lie in the appreciation of means towards an acknowledged end, but in the indifference of persons in general to the end itself. If it were felt that the free development of individuality is one of the leading essentials of well-being; that it is not only a coordinate element with all that is designated by the terms *civilization, instruction, education, culture,* but is itself a necessary part and condition of all those things, there would be no danger that liberty should be undervalued, and the adjustment of the boundaries between it and social control would present no extraordinary difficulty. But the evil is that individual spontaneity is hardly recognized by the common modes of thinking as having any intrinsic worth or deserving any regard on its own account. The majority, being satisfied with the ways of mankind as they now are (for it is they who make them what they are), cannot comprehend why those ways should not be good enough for everybody; and what is more, spontaneity forms no part of the ideal of the majority of moral and social reformers, but is rather looked on with jealousy, as a troublesome and perhaps rebellious obstruction to the general acceptance of what these reformers, in their own judgment, think would be best for mankind. Few persons, out of Germany, even comprehend the meaning of the doctrine which Wilhelm von Humboldt, so eminent both as a *savant*[2] and as a politician, made the text of a treatise—that "the end of man, or that which is prescribed by the eternal or immutable dictates of reason, and not suggested by vague and transient desires, is the highest and most harmonious development of his powers to a complete and consistent whole;" that, therefore, the object "towards which every human being must ceaselessly direct his efforts, and on which especially those who design to influence their fellow-men must ever keep their eyes, is the individuality of power and development;" that for this there are two requisites, "freedom, and variety* of situations;" and that from the union of these arise "individual vigour and manifold diversity," which combine themselves in "originality."†

Little, however, as people are accustomed to a doctrine like that of von Humboldt, and surprising as it may be to them to find so high a value attached to individuality, the question, one must nevertheless think, can only be one of degree. No one's idea of excellence in conduct is that people should do absolutely nothing but copy one another. No one would assert that people ought not to put into their mode of life, and into the conduct of their concerns, any impress whatever of their own judgment or of their own individual character. On the other hand, it would be absurd to pretend that people ought to live as if nothing whatever had been known in the world before they came into it; as if experience had as yet done nothing towards showing that one mode of existence, or of conduct, is preferable to another. Nobody denies that people should be so taught and trained in youth as to know and benefit by the ascertained results of human experience. But it is the privilege and proper condition of a human being, arrived at the maturity of his faculties, to use and interpret experience in his own way. It is for him to find out what part of recorded experience is properly applicable to his own circumstances and character. The traditions and customs of other people are, to a certain extent, evidence of what their experience has taught *them*—presumptive evidence, and as such, have a claim to this deference. But, in the first place, their experience may be too narrow, or they may not have interpreted it rightly. Secondly, their interpretation of experience may be correct but unsuitable to him. Customs are made for customary circumstances and customary characters; and his circumstances or his character may be uncustomary. Thirdly, though the customs are both good as customs and suitable to

---

* freedom, and variety—freedom, and a variety (1859a, 1859b)
† *The Sphere and Duties of Government*, from the German of Baron Wilhelm von Humboldt, pp. 11-13.

him, yet to conform to custom merely *as* custom does not educate or develop in him any of the qualities which are the distinctive endowment of a human being. The human faculties of perception, judgment, discriminative feeling, mental activity, and even moral preference are exercised only in making a choice. He who does anything because it is the custom makes no choice. He gains no practice either in discerning or in desiring what is best. The mental and moral, like the muscular powers, are improved only by being used. The faculties are called into no exercise by doing a thing merely because others do it, no more than by believing a thing only because others believe it. If the grounds of an opinion are not conclusive to the person's own reason, his reason cannot be strengthened, but is likely to be weakened by his adopting it: and if the inducements to an act are not such as are consentaneous to[3] his own feelings and character (where affection, or the rights of others, are not concerned), it is so much done towards rendering his feelings and character inert and torpid instead of active and energetic.

He who lets the world, or his own portion of it, choose his plan of life for him has no need of any other faculty than the ape-like one of imitation. He who chooses his plan for himself employs all his faculties. He must use observation to see, reasoning and judgment to foresee, activity to gather materials for decision, discrimination to decide, and when he has decided, firmness and self-control to hold to his deliberate decision. And these qualities he requires and exercises exactly in proportion as the part of his conduct which he determines according to his own judgment and feelings is a large one. It is possible that he might be guided in some good path, and kept out of harm's way, without any of these things. But what will be his comparative worth as a human being? It really is of importance, not only what men do, but also what manner of men they are that do it. Among the works of man, which human life is rightly employed in perfecting and beautifying, the first in importance surely is man himself. Supposing it were possible to get houses built, corn grown, battles fought, causes tried, and even churches erected and prayers said by machinery—by automatons in human form—it would be a considerable loss to exchange for these automatons even the men and women who at present inhabit the more civilized parts of the world, and who assuredly are but starved specimens of what nature can and will produce. Human nature is not a machine to be built after a model, and set to do exactly the work prescribed for it, but a tree, which requires to grow and develop itself on all sides according to the tendency of the inward forces which make it a living thing.

It will probably be conceded that it is desirable people should exercise their understandings, and that an intelligent following of custom, or even occasionally an intelligent deviation from custom, is better than a blind and simply mechanical adhesion to it. To a certain extent it is admitted that our understanding should be our own; but there is not the same willingness to admit that our desires and impulses should be our own likewise, or that to possess impulses of our own, and of any strength, is anything but a peril and a snare. Yet desires and impulses are as much a part of a perfect human being as beliefs and restraints; and strong impulses are only perilous when not properly balanced, when one set of aims and inclinations is developed into strength, while others, which ought to co-exist with them, remain weak and inactive. It is not because men's desires are strong that they act ill; it is because their consciences are weak. There is no natural connection between strong impulses and a weak conscience. The natural connection is the other way. To say that one person's desires and feelings are stronger and more various than those of another is merely to say that he has more of the raw material of human nature, and is therefore capable, perhaps of more evil, but certainly of more good. Strong impulses are but another name for energy. Energy may be turned to bad uses; but more good may always be made of an energetic nature than of an indolent and impassive one. Those who have most natural feeling are always those whose cultivated feelings may be made the strongest. The same strong susceptibilities which make the personal impulses vivid and powerful are also the source from where are generated the most passionate love of virtue and the sternest self-control. It is through the cultivation of these that society both does its duty and protects its interests; not by rejecting the stuff of which heroes are made, because it knows not how to make them. A person whose desires and impulses are his own—are the expression of his own nature, as it has been developed and modified by his own culture—is said to have a character. One whose desires and impulses are not his own has no character, no more than a steam-engine has a character. If, in addition to being his own, his impulses are strong and are under the government of a strong will, he has an energetic character. Whoever thinks that individuality of desires and impulses should not be encouraged to unfold itself must maintain that society has no need of strong natures—is not the better for containing many persons who have much character—and that a high general average of energy is not desirable.

In some early states of society, these forces might be, and were, too much ahead of the power which society then possessed of disciplining and controlling them. There has been a time when the element of spontaneity and individuality was in excess, and the social principle had a hard struggle with it. The difficulty then was to induce men of strong bodies or minds to pay obedience to any rules which required them to control their impulses. To overcome this difficulty, law and discipline, like the Popes struggling against the Emperors, asserted a power over the whole man, claiming to control all his life in order to control his character—which society had not found any other sufficient means of binding. But society has now fairly got the better of individuality; and the danger which threatens human nature is not the excess, but the deficiency, of personal impulses and preferences. Things are vastly changed since the passions of those who were strong by station or by personal endowment were in a state of habitual rebellion against laws and ordinances and required to be rigorously chained up to enable the persons within their reach to enjoy any particle of security. In our times, from the highest class of society down to the lowest, everyone lives as under the eye of a hostile and dreaded censorship. Not only in what concerns others, but in what concerns only themselves, the individual or the family do not ask themselves: what do I prefer? or, what would suit my character and disposition? or, what would allow the best and highest in me to have fair play, and enable it to grow and thrive? They ask themselves: what is suitable to my position? what is usually done by persons of my station and pecuniary circumstances? or (worse still) what is usually done by persons of a station and circumstances superior to mine? I do not mean that they choose what is customary in preference to what suits their own inclination. It does not occur to them to have any inclination except for what is customary. Thus the mind itself is bowed to the yoke: even in what people do for pleasure, conformity is the first thing thought of; they like in crowds;[4] they exercise choice only among things commonly done; peculiarity of taste [and] eccentricity of conduct are shunned equally with crimes, until by dint of not following their own nature, they have no nature to follow: their human capacities are withered and starved; they become incapable of any strong wishes or native pleasures, and are generally without either opinions or feelings of home growth, or properly their own. Now is this, or is it not, the desirable condition of human nature?

It is so, on the Calvinistic theory. According to that, the one great offense of man is self-will. All the good of which humanity is capable is comprised in obedience. You have no choice; thus you must do, and not otherwise: "whatever is not a duty, is a sin." Human nature being radically corrupt, there is no redemption for anyone until human nature is killed within him. To one holding this theory of life, crushing out any of the human faculties, capacities, and susceptibilities is no evil: man needs no capacity but that of surrendering himself to the will of God; and if he uses any of his faculties for any other purpose but to do that supposed will more effectually, he is better without them. This* is the theory of Calvinism; and it is held, in a mitigated form, by many who do not consider themselves Calvinists—the mitigation consisting in giving a less ascetic interpretation to the alleged will of God, asserting it to be his will that mankind should gratify some of their inclinations, of course not in the manner they themselves prefer, but in the way of obedience, that is, in a way prescribed to them by authority, and, therefore, by the necessary conditions of the case, the same for all.

In some such insidious form there is at present a strong tendency to this narrow theory of life, and to the pinched and hidebound type of human character which it patronizes. Many persons, no doubt, sincerely think that human beings thus cramped and dwarfed are as their Maker designed them to be; just as many have thought that trees are a much finer thing when clipped into pollards,[5] or cut out into figures of animals, than as nature made them. But if it is any part of religion to believe that man was made by a good Being,† it is more consistent with that faith to believe that this Being gave all human faculties that they might be cultivated and unfolded, not rooted out and consumed, and that he takes delight in every nearer approach made by his creatures to the ideal conception embodied in them, every increase in any of their capabilities of comprehension, of action, or of enjoyment. There is a different type of human excellence from the Calvinistic—a conception of humanity as having its nature bestowed on it for other purposes than merely to be abnegated. "Pagan self-assertion" is one of the elements of human worth, as well as "Christian self-denial."‡ There is a Greek ideal of self-development, which the Platonic and Christian ideal of self-government blends with, but does not supersede. It may be better to be a John Knox than an Alcibiades, but it is better to be a Pericles than either; nor would a Pericles, if we had one in these days, be without anything good which belonged to John Knox.[6]

---

* This—That (1859a, 1859b).
† Being—being (1859a, 1859b)
‡ Sterling's *Essays*. [Editor: John Sterling's (1806-1844) *Essays and Tales* (London; 2 vols., 1848).]

It is not by wearing down into uniformity all that is individual in themselves, but by cultivating it and calling it forth, within the limits imposed by the rights and interests of others, that human beings become a noble and beautiful object of contemplation; and as the works partake the character of those who do them, by the same process human life also becomes rich, diversified, and animating, furnishing more abundant aliment[7] to high thoughts and elevating feelings, and strengthening the tie which binds every individual to the race, by making the race infinitely better worth belonging to. In proportion to the development of his individuality, each person becomes more valuable to himself, and is therefore capable of being more valuable to others. There is a greater fullness of life about his own existence, and when there is more life in the units there is more in the mass which is composed of them. As much compression as is necessary to prevent the stronger specimens of human nature from encroaching on the rights of others cannot be dispensed with; but for this there is ample compensation even in the point of view of human development. The means of development which the individual loses by being prevented from gratifying his inclinations to the injury of others are chiefly obtained at the expense of the development of other people. And even to himself there is a full equivalent in the better development of the social part of his nature, rendered possible by the restraint put upon the selfish part. To be held to rigid rules of justice for the sake of others develops the feelings and capacities which have the good of others for their object. But to be restrained in things not affecting their good, by their mere displeasure, develops nothing valuable except such force of character as may unfold itself in resisting the restraint. If acquiesced in, it dulls and blunts the whole nature. To give any fair play to the nature of each, it is essential that different persons should be allowed to lead different lives. In proportion as this latitude has been exercised in any age has that age been noteworthy to posterity. Even despotism does not produce its worst effects, so long as individuality exists under it; and whatever crushes individuality is despotism, by whatever name it may be called, and whether it professes to be enforcing the will of God or the injunctions of men.

Having said that individuality is the same thing with development, and that it is only the cultivation of individuality which produces, or can produce, well-developed human beings, I might here close the argument; for what more or better can be said of any condition of human affairs than that it brings human beings themselves nearer to the best thing they can be? Or what worse can be said of any obstruction to good than that it prevents this? Doubtless, however, these considerations will not suffice to convince those who most need convincing; and it is necessary further to show that these developed human beings are of some use to the undeveloped—to point out to those who do not desire liberty, and would not avail themselves of it, that they may be in some intelligible manner rewarded for allowing other people to make use of it without hindrance.

In the first place, then, I would suggest that they might possibly learn something from them. It will not be denied by anybody that originality is a valuable element in human affairs. There is always need of persons not only to discover new truths and point out when what were once truths are true no longer, but also to commence new practices and set the example of more enlightened conduct and better taste and sense in human life. This cannot well be gainsaid by anybody who does not believe that the world has already attained perfection in all its ways and practices. It is true that this benefit is not capable of being rendered by everybody alike; there are but few persons, in comparison with the whole of mankind, whose experiments, if adopted by others, would be likely to be any improvement on established practice. But these few are the salt of the earth; without them, human life would become a stagnant pool. Not only is it they who introduce good things which did not before exist; it is they who keep the life in those which already existed. If there were nothing new to be done, would human intellect cease to be necessary? Would it be a reason why those who do the old things should forget why they are done, and do them like cattle, not like human beings? There is only too great a tendency in the best beliefs and practices to degenerate into the mechanical; and unless there were a succession of persons whose ever-recurring originality prevents the grounds of those beliefs and practices from becoming merely traditional, such dead matter would not resist the smallest shock from anything really alive, and there would be no reason why civilization should not die out, as in the Byzantine Empire.[8] Persons of genius, it is true, are, and are always likely to be, a small minority; but in order to have them, it is necessary to preserve the soil in which they grow. Genius can only breathe freely in an *atmosphere of freedom.* Persons of genius are, *ex vi termini,*[9] *more* individual than any other people—less capable, consequently, of fitting themselves, without hurtful compression, into any of the small number of molds which society provides in order to save its members the trouble of forming their own character. If from timidity they consent to be forced into one of these molds, and to let all that part of themselves which cannot expand under the pressure remain unexpanded, society will be little the better for their genius. If they are of a strong character and break their fetters, they become a mark for the society which has not succeeded in reducing them to commonplace, to point at with solemn warning as "wild," "erratic," and the like—much as if one should complain of the Niagara river[10] for not flowing smoothly between its banks like a Dutch canal.

I insist thus emphatically on the importance of genius and the necessity of allowing it to unfold itself freely both in thought and in practice, being well aware that no one will deny the position in theory, but knowing also that almost everyone, in reality, is totally indifferent to it. People think genius a fine thing if it enables a man to write an exciting poem or paint a picture. But in its true sense, that of originality in thought and action, though no one says that it is not a thing to be admired, nearly all, at heart, think they can do very well without it. Unhappily this is too natural to be wondered at. Originality is the one thing which unoriginal minds cannot feel the use of. They cannot see what it is to do for them—how should they? If they could see what it would do for them, it would not be originality. The first service which originality has to render them is that of opening their eyes; which being once fully done, they would have a chance of being themselves original. Meanwhile, recollecting that nothing was ever yet done which someone was not the first to do, and that all good things which exist are the fruits of originality, let them be modest enough to believe that there is something still left for it to accomplish, and assure themselves that they are more in need of originality, the less they are conscious of the want.

In sober truth, whatever homage may be professed, or even paid, to real or supposed mental superiority, the general tendency of things throughout the world is to render mediocrity the ascendant power among mankind. In ancient history, in the Middle Ages, and in a diminishing degree through the long transition from feudality to the present time, the individual was a power in himself; and if he had either great talents or a high social position, he was a considerable power. At present individuals are lost in the crowd. In politics it is almost a triviality to say that public opinion now rules the world. The only power deserving the name is that of masses, and of governments while they make themselves the organ of the tendencies and instincts of masses. This is as true in the moral and social relations of private life as in public transactions. Those whose opinions go by the name of public opinion are not always the same sort of public: in America they are the whole white population; in England, chiefly the middle class. But they are always a mass, that is to say, collective mediocrity. And what is still greater novelty, the mass do not now take their opinions from dignitaries in church or state, from ostensible leaders, or from books. Their thinking is done for them by men much like themselves, addressing them or speaking in their name, on the spur of the moment, through the newspapers. I am not complaining of all this. I do not assert that anything better is compatible, as a general rule, with the present low state of the human mind. But that does not hinder the government of mediocrity from being mediocre government. No government by a democracy or a numerous aristocracy, either in its political acts or in the opinions, qualities, and tone of mind which it fosters, ever did or could rise above mediocrity, except in so far as the sovereign Many have let themselves be guided (which in their best times they always have done) by the counsels and influence of a more highly gifted and instructed One or Few. The initiation of all wise or noble things comes and must come from individuals; generally at first from some one individual. The honor and glory of the average man is that he is capable of following that initiative; that he can respond internally to wise and noble things, and be led to them with his eyes open. I am not countenancing the sort of "hero-worship" which applauds the strong man of genius for forcibly seizing on the government of the world and making it do his bidding in spite of itself.[11] All he can claim is freedom to point out the way. The power of compelling others into it is not only inconsistent with the freedom and development of all the rest, but corrupting to the strong man himself. It does seem, however, that when the opinions of masses of merely average men are everywhere become or becoming the dominant power, the counterpoise and corrective to that tendency would be the more and more pronounced individuality of those who stand on the higher eminences of thought. It is in these circumstances most especially that exceptional individuals, instead of being deterred, should be encouraged in acting differently from the mass. In other times there was no advantage in their doing so, unless they acted not only differently, but better. In this age the mere example of nonconformity, the mere refusal to bend the knee to custom, is itself a service. Precisely because the tyranny of opinion is such as to make eccentricity a reproach, it is desirable, in order to break through that tyranny, that people should be eccentric. Eccentricity has always abounded when and where strength of character has abounded; and the amount of eccentricity in a society has generally been proportional to the amount of genius, mental vigor, and moral courage which it contained. That so few now dare to be eccentric marks the chief danger of the time.

I have said that it is important to give the freest scope possible to uncustomary things, in order that it may in time appear which of these are fit to be converted into customs. But independence of action and disregard of custom are not solely deserving of encouragement for the chance they afford that better modes of action, and customs more worthy of general adoption, may be struck out; nor is it only persons of decided mental superiority who have a just claim to carry on their lives in their own way. There is no reason that all human existence* should be constructed on some one or some small number of patterns. If a person possesses any tolerable amount of common sense and experience, his own mode of laying out his existence is the best, not because it is the best in itself, but because it is his own mode. Human beings are not like sheep; and even sheep are not indistinguishably alike. A man cannot get a coat or a pair of boots to fit him unless they are either made to his measure or he has a whole warehouse full to choose from; and is it easier to fit him with a life than with a coat, or are human beings more like one another in their whole physical and spiritual conformation than in the shape of their feet? If it were only that people have diversities of taste, that is reason enough for not attempting to shape them all after one model. But different persons also require different conditions for their spiritual development, and can no more exist healthily in the same moral, than all the variety of plants can in the same physical, atmosphere and climate. The same things which are helps to one person towards the cultivation of his higher nature are hindrances to another. The same mode of life is a healthy excitement to one, keeping all his faculties of action and enjoyment in their best order, while to another it is a distracting burden, which suspends or crushes all internal life. Such are the differences among human beings in their sources of pleasure, their susceptibilities of pain, and the operation on them of different physical and moral agencies, that unless there is a corresponding diversity in their modes of life, they neither obtain their fair share of happiness, nor grow up to the mental, moral, and aesthetic stature of which their nature is capable. Why then should tolerance, as far as the public sentiment is concerned, extend only to tastes and modes of life which extort acquiescence by the multitude of their adherents? Nowhere (except in some monastic institutions) is diversity of taste entirely unrecognized; a person may, without blame, either like or dislike rowing, or smoking, or music, or

---

* existence—existences (1859a, 1859b).

athletic exercises, or chess, or cards, or study, because both those who like each of these things, and those who dislike them, are too numerous to be put down. But the man, and still more the woman, who can be accused either of doing "what nobody does," or of not doing "what everybody does," is the subject of as much depreciatory remark as if he or she had committed some grave moral delinquency. Persons require to possess a title, or some other badge of rank, or the consideration of people of rank, to be able to indulge somewhat in the luxury of doing as they like without detriment to their estimation. To indulge somewhat, I repeat: for whoever allow themselves much of that indulgence incur the risk of something worse than disparaging speeches—they are in peril of a commission *de lunatico*[12] and of having their property taken from them and given to their relations.*

There is one characteristic of the present direction of public opinion peculiarly calculated to make it intolerant of any marked demonstration of individuality. The general average of mankind are not only moderate in intellect, but also moderate in inclinations; they have no tastes or wishes strong enough to incline them to do anything unusual, and they consequently do not understand those who have, and class all such with the wild and intemperate whom they are accustomed to look down upon. Now, in addition to this fact which is general, we have only to suppose that a strong movement has set in towards the improvement of

---

* There is something both contemptible and frightful in the sort of evidence on which, of late years, any person can be judicially declared unfit for the management of his affairs; and after his death, his disposal of his property can be set aside if there is enough of it to pay the expenses of litigation—which are charged on the property itself. All of the minute details of his daily life are pried into, and whatever is found which, seen through the medium of the perceiving and describing faculties of the lowest of the low, bears an appearance unlike absolute commonplace is laid before the jury as evidence of insanity, and often with success; the jurors being little, if at all, less vulgar and ignorant than the witnesses, while the judges, with that extraordinary want of knowledge of human nature and life which continually astonishes us in English lawyers, often help to mislead them. These trials speak volumes as to the state of feeling and opinion among the vulgar with regard to human liberty. So far from setting any value on individuality—so far from respecting the right [rights 1859a, 1859b] of each individual to act, in things indifferent, as seems good to his own judgment and inclinations, judges and juries cannot even conceive that a person in a state of sanity can desire such freedom. In former days, when it was proposed to burn atheists, charitable people used to suggest putting them in a madhouse instead; it would be nothing surprising nowadays were we to see this done, and the doers applauding themselves because, instead of persecuting for religion, they had adopted so humane and Christian a mode of treating these unfortunates, not without a silent satisfaction at their having thereby obtained their deserts.

morals, and it is evident what we have to expect. In these days such a movement has set in; much has actually been effected in the way of increased regularity of conduct and discouragement of excesses; and there is a philanthropic spirit abroad, for the exercise of which there is no more inviting field than the moral and prudential improvement of our fellow creatures. These tendencies of the times cause the public to be more disposed than at most former periods to prescribe general rules of conduct and endeavor to make everyone conform to the approved standard. And that standard, express or tacit, is to desire nothing strongly. Its ideal of character is to be without any marked character—to maim by compression, like a Chinese lady's foot,[13] every part of human nature which stands out prominently and tends to make the person markedly dissimilar in outline to commonplace humanity.

As is usually the case with ideals which exclude one-half of what is desirable, the present standard of approbation produces only an inferior imitation of the other half. Instead of great energies guided by vigorous reason, and strong feelings strongly controlled by a conscientious will, its result is weak feelings and weak energies, which therefore can be kept in outward conformity to rule without any strength either of will or of reason. Already energetic characters on any large scale are becoming merely traditional. There is now scarcely any outlet for energy in this country except business. The energy expended in this* may still be regarded as considerable. What little is left from that employment is expended on some hobby, which may be a useful, even a philanthropic, hobby, but is always some one thing, and generally a thing of small dimensions. The greatness of England is now all collective; individually small, we only appear capable of anything great by our habit of combining; and with this our moral and religious philanthropists are perfectly contented. But it was men of another stamp than this that made England what it has been; and men of another stamp will be needed to prevent its decline.

The despotism of custom is everywhere the standing hindrance to human advancement, being in unceasing antagonism to that disposition to aim at something better than customary, which is called, according to circumstances, the *spirit of liberty*, or that of *progress* or *improvement*. The spirit of improvement is not always a spirit of liberty, for it may aim at forcing improvements on an unwilling people; and the spirit of liberty, in so far as it resists such attempts, may ally itself locally and temporarily

---

* this—that (1859a, 1859b).

with the opponents of improvement; but the only unfailing and permanent source of improvement is liberty, since by it there are as many possible independent centers of improvement as there are individuals. The progressive principle, however, in either shape, whether as the love of liberty or of improvement, is antagonistic to the sway of custom, involving at least emancipation from that yoke; and the contest between the two constitutes the chief interest of the history of mankind. The greater part of the world has, properly speaking, no history, because the despotism of custom is complete. This is the case over the whole East. Custom is there, in all things, the final appeal; *justice* and *right* mean conformity to custom; the argument of custom no one, unless some tyrant intoxicated with power, thinks of resisting. And we see the result. Those nations must once have had originality; they did not start out of the ground populous, lettered, and versed in many of the arts of life; they made themselves all this, and were then the greatest and most powerful nations of* the world. What are they now? The subjects or dependents of tribes whose forefathers wandered in the forests when theirs had magnificent palaces and gorgeous temples, but over whom custom exercised only a divided rule with liberty and progress. A people, it appears, may be progressive for a certain length of time, and then stop. When does it stop? When it ceases to possess individuality. If a similar change should befall the nations of Europe, it will not be in exactly the same shape: the despotism of custom with which these nations are threatened is not precisely stationariness. It proscribes singularity, but it does not preclude change, provided all change together. We have discarded the fixed costumes of our forefathers; everyone must still dress like other people, but the fashion may change once or twice a year. We thus take care that when there is change it shall be for change's sake, and not from any idea of beauty or convenience; for the same idea of beauty or convenience would not strike all the world at the same moment, and be simultaneously thrown aside by all at another moment. But we are progressive as well as changeable: we continually make new inventions in mechanical things, and keep them until they are again superseded by better; we are eager for improvement in politics, in education, even in morals, though in this last our idea of improvement chiefly consists in persuading or forcing other people to be as good as ourselves. It is not progress that we object to; on the contrary, we flatter ourselves that we are the most progressive people who

---

* of—in (1859a, 1859b).

ever lived. It is individuality that we war against: we should think we had done wonders if we had made ourselves all alike, forgetting that the unlikeness of one person to another is generally the first thing which draws the attention of either to the imperfection of his own type and the superiority of another, or the possibility, by combining the advantages of both, of producing something better than either. We have a warning example in China—a nation of much talent, and, in some respects, even wisdom, owing to the rare good fortune of having been provided at an early period with a particularly good set of customs, the work, in some measure, of men to whom even the most enlightened European must accord, under certain limitations, the title of sages and philosophers. They are remarkable, too, in the excellence of their apparatus for impressing, as far as possible, the best wisdom they possess upon every mind in the community, and securing that those who have appropriated most of it shall occupy the posts of honor and power. Surely the people who did this have discovered the secret of human progressiveness and must have kept themselves steadily at the head of the movement of the world. On the contrary, they have become stationary—have remained so for thousands of years; and if they are ever to be further improved, it must be by foreigners. They have succeeded beyond all hope in what English philanthropists are so industriously working at—in making a people all alike, all governing their thoughts and conduct by the same maxims and rules; and these are the fruits. The modern *régime* of public opinion is, in an unorganized form, what the Chinese educational and political systems are in an organized; and unless individuality shall be able successfully to assert itself against this yoke, Europe, notwithstanding its noble antecedents and its professed Christianity, will tend to become another China.

What is it that has till now preserved Europe from this lot? What has made the European family of nations an improving, instead of a stationary portion of mankind? Not any superior excellence in them, which when it exists, exists as the effect, not as the cause; but their remarkable diversity of character and culture. Individuals, classes, [and] nations have been extremely unlike one another: they have struck out a great variety of paths, each leading to something valuable; and although at every period those who traveled in different paths have been intolerant of one another, and each would have thought it an excellent thing if all the rest could have been compelled to travel his road, their attempts to thwart each other's development have rarely had any permanent success, and each has in time endured to receive the good which the others have offered. Europe is, in my judgment, wholly indebted to this plurality of paths for its progressive and many-sided development. But it already begins to possess this benefit in a considerably less degree. It is decidedly advancing towards the Chinese ideal of making all people alike. M. de Tocqueville, in his last important work,[14] remarks how much more the Frenchmen of the present day resemble one another than did those even of the last generation. The same remark might be made of Englishmen in a far greater degree. In a passage already quoted from Wilhelm von Humboldt,[15] he points out two things as necessary conditions of human development, because necessary to render people unlike one another— namely, freedom and variety of situations. The second of these two conditions is in this country every day diminishing. The circumstances which surround different classes and individuals, and shape their characters, are daily becoming more assimilated. Formerly, different ranks, different neighborhoods, different trades and professions lived in what might be called different worlds; at present, to a great degree in the same. Comparatively speaking, they now read the same things, listen to the same things, see the same things, go to the same places, have their hopes and fears directed to the same objects, have the same rights and liberties, and the same means of asserting them. Great as are the differences of position which remain, they are nothing to those which have ceased. And the assimilation is still proceeding. All the political changes of the age promote it, since they all tend to raise the low and to lower the high. Every extension of education promotes it, because education brings people under common influences, and gives them access to the general stock of facts and sentiments. Improvements in the means of communication promote it, by bringing the inhabitants of distant places into personal contact, and keeping up a rapid flow of changes of residence between one place and another. The increase of commerce and manufactures promotes it, by diffusing more widely the advantages of easy circumstances and opening all objects of ambition, even the highest, to general competition, whereby the desire of rising becomes no longer the character of a particular class, but of all classes. A more powerful agency than even all these, in bringing about a general similarity among mankind, is the complete establishment, in this and other free countries, of the ascendancy of public opinion in the state. As the various social eminences which enabled persons entrenched on them to disregard the opinion of the multitude gradually became leveled; as the very idea of resisting the will of the public, when it is positively known that they have a will, disappears more and more from the minds of practical politicians, there ceases to be any social support for nonconformity—any substantive power in society, which, itself opposed to the ascendancy of numbers, is interested in taking under its protection opinions and tendencies at variance with those of the public.

The combination of all these causes forms so great a mass of influences hostile to individuality that it is not easy to see how it can stand its ground. It will do so with increasing difficulty unless the intelligent part of the public can be made to feel its value—to see that it is good there should be differences, even though not for the better, even though, as it may appear to them, some should be for the worse. If the claims of individuality are ever to be asserted, the time is now, while much is still wanting to complete the enforced assimilation. It is only in the earlier stages that any stand can be successfully made against the encroachment. The demand that all other people shall resemble ourselves grows by what it feeds on. If resistance waits till life is reduced *nearly* to one uniform type, all deviations from that type will come to be considered impious, immoral, even monstrous and contrary to nature. Mankind speedily become unable to conceive diversity when they have been for some time unaccustomed to see it.

CHAPTER IV

Of the Limits to the Authority of Society over the Individual

WHAT, then, is the rightful limit to the sovereignty of the individual over himself? Where does the authority of society begin? How much of human life should be assigned to individuality, and how much to society?

Each will receive its proper share if each has that which more particularly concerns it. To individuality should belong the part of life in which it is chiefly the individual that is interested; to society, the part which chiefly interests society.

Though society is not founded on a contract, and though no good purpose is answered by inventing a contract in order to deduce social obligations from it,[1] everyone who receives the protection of society owes a return for the benefit, and the fact of living in society renders it indispensable that each should be bound to observe a certain line of conduct towards the rest. This conduct consists, first, in not injuring the interests of one another, or rather certain interests which, either by express legal provision or by tacit understanding, ought to be considered as rights; and, secondly, in each person's bearing his share (to be fixed on some equitable principle) of the labors and sacrifices incurred for defending the society or its members from injury and molestation. These conditions society is justified in enforcing at all costs to those who endeavor to withhold fulfillment. Nor is this all that society may do. The acts of an individual may be hurtful to others, or wanting in due consideration for their welfare, without going the length of violating any of their constituted rights. The offender may then be justly punished by opinion, though not by law. As soon as any part of a person's conduct affects prejudicially the interests of others, society has jurisdiction over it, and the question whether the general welfare will or will not be promoted by interfering with it becomes open to discussion. But there is no room for entertaining any such question when a person's conduct affects the interests of no persons besides himself, or needs not affect them unless they like (all the persons concerned being of full age and the ordinary amount of understanding). In all such cases there should be perfect freedom, legal and social, to do the action and stand the consequences.

It would be a great misunderstanding of this doctrine to suppose that it is one of selfish indifference which pretends that human beings have no business with each other's conduct in life, and that they should not concern themselves about the well-doing or well-being of one another, unless their own interest is involved. Instead of any diminution, there is need of a great increase of disinterested exertion to promote the good of others. But disinterested benevolence can find other instruments to persuade people to their good than whips and scourges, either of the literal or the metaphorical sort. I am the last person to undervalue the self-regarding virtues; they are only second in importance, if even second, to the social. It is equally the business of education to cultivate both. But even education works by conviction and persuasion as well as by compulsion, and it is by the former only that, when the period of education is past, the self-regarding virtues should be inculcated. Human beings owe to each other help to distinguish the better from the worse, and encouragement to choose the former and avoid the latter. They should be forever stimulating each other to increased exercise of their higher faculties and increased direction of their feelings and aims towards wise instead of foolish, elevating instead of degrading, objects and contemplations. But neither one person, nor any number of persons, is warranted in saying to another human creature of ripe years that he shall not do with his life for his own benefit what he chooses to do with it. He is the person most interested in his own well-being—the interest which any other person, except in cases of strong personal attachment, can have in it is trifling compared with that which he himself has; the interest which society has in him individually (except as to his conduct to others) is fractional and altogether indirect, while with respect to his own feelings and circumstances, the most ordinary man or woman has means of knowledge immeasurably surpassing those that can be possessed by anyone else. The interference of society to overrule his judgment and purposes in what only regards himself must be grounded on general presumptions which may be altogether wrong and, even if right, are as likely as not to be mis-applied to individual cases by persons no better acquainted with the cir-cumstances of such cases than those are who look at them merely from without. In this department, therefore, of human affairs, individuality has its proper field of action. In the conduct of human beings towards one another, it is necessary that general rules should for the most part be observed in order that people may know what they have to expect; but in each person's own concerns, his individual spontaneity is entitled to free exercise. Considerations to aid his judgment [and] exhortations to strengthen his will may be offered to him, even obtruded[2] on him, by others; but he himself is the final judge. All errors which he is likely to commit against advice and warning are far outweighed by the evil of allowing others to constrain him to what they deem his good.

I do not mean that the feelings with which a person is regarded by others ought not to be in any way affected by his self-regarding qualities or deficiencies. This is neither possible nor desirable. If he is eminent in any of the qualities which conduce to his own good, he is, so far, a proper object of admiration. He is so much the nearer to the ideal perfec-tion of human nature. If he is grossly deficient in those qualities, a senti-ment the opposite of admiration will follow. There is a degree of folly, and a degree of what may be called (though the phrase is not unobjec-tionable) lowness or depravation of taste, which, though it cannot justify doing harm to the person who manifests it, renders him necessarily and properly a subject of distaste, or, in extreme cases, even of contempt: a person could not have the opposite qualities in due strength without entertaining these feelings. Though doing no wrong to anyone, a person may so act as to compel us to judge him, and feel to him, as a fool or as a being of an inferior order; and since this judgment and feeling are a fact which he would prefer to avoid, it is doing him a service to warn him of it beforehand, as of any other disagreeable consequence to which he exposes himself. It would be well, indeed, if this good office were much more freely rendered than the common notions of politeness at present permit, and if one person could honestly point out to another that he thinks him in fault, without being considered unmannerly or presuming. We have a right, also, in various ways, to act upon our unfavorable opin-ion of anyone, not to the oppression of his individuality, but in the exer-cise of ours. We are not bound, for example, to seek his society; we have a right to avoid it (though not to parade the avoidance), for we have a right to choose the society most acceptable to us. We have a right, and it may be our duty, to caution others against him if we think his example or conversation likely to have a pernicious effect on those with whom he associates. We may give others a preference over him in optional good offices, except those which tend to his improvement. In these various modes a person may suffer very severe penalties at the hands of others for faults which directly concern only himself; but he suffers these penalties only in so far as they are the natural and, as it were, the spontaneous consequences of the faults themselves, not because they are purposely inflicted on him for the sake of punishment. A person who shows rashness, obstinacy, self-conceit—who cannot live within moderate means; who cannot restrain himself from hurtful indulgences; who pursues animal pleasures at the expense of those of feeling and intellect—must expect to be lowered in the opinion of others, and to have a less share of their favorable sentiments; but of this he has no right to complain unless he has merited their favor by special excellence in his social relations and has thus established a title to their good offices, which is not affected by his demerits towards himself.

What I contend for is that the inconveniences which are strictly inseparable from the unfavorable judgment of others are the only ones to which a person should ever be subjected for that portion of his conduct and character which concerns his own good, but which does not affect the interests of others in their relations with him. Acts injurious to others require a totally different treatment. Encroachment on their rights; infliction on them of any loss or damage not justified by his own rights; falsehood or duplicity in dealing with them; unfair or ungenerous use of advantages over them; even selfish abstinence from defending them against injury—these are fit objects of moral reprobation and, in grave cases, of moral retribution and punishment. And not only these acts, but the dispositions which lead to them, are properly immoral and fit subjects of disapprobation which may rise to abhorrence. Cruelty of disposition; malice and ill-nature; that most anti-social and odious of all passions, envy; dissimulation and insincerity; irascibility on insufficient cause, and resentment disproportioned to the provocation; the love of domineering over others; the desire to engross more than one's share of advantages (the *pleonexia*[3] of the Greeks); the pride which derives gratification from the abasement of others; the egotism which thinks self and its concerns more important than everything else, and decides all doubtful questions in his own favor—these are moral vices and constitute a bad and odious moral character; unlike the self-regarding faults previously mentioned, which are not properly immoralities, and to whatever pitch they may be carried, do not constitute wickedness. They may be proofs of any amount of folly, or want of personal dignity and self-respect; but they are only a subject of moral reprobation when they involve a breach of duty to others, for whose sake the individual is bound to have care for himself. What are called duties to ourselves are not socially obligatory unless circumstances render them at the same time duties to others. The term *duty to oneself*, when it means anything more than prudence, means self-respect or self-development; and for none of these is anyone accountable to his fellow-creatures, because for none of them is it for the good of mankind that he is held accountable to them.

The distinction between the loss of consideration which a person may rightly incur by defect of prudence or of personal dignity, and the reprobation which is due to him for an offense against the rights of others, is not a merely nominal distinction. It makes a vast difference both in our feelings and in our conduct towards him whether he displeases us in things in which we think we have a right to control him or in things in which we know that we have not. If he displeases us, we may express our distaste, and we may stand aloof from a person as well as from a thing that displeases us; but we shall not therefore feel called on to make his life uncomfortable. We shall reflect that he already bears, or will bear, the whole penalty of his error; if he spoils his life by mismanagement, we shall not, for that reason, desire to spoil it still further—instead of wishing to punish him, we shall rather endeavor to alleviate his punishment by showing him how he may avoid or cure the evils his conduct tends to bring upon him. He may be to us an object of pity, perhaps of dislike, but not of anger or resentment; we shall not treat him like an enemy of society—the worst we shall think ourselves justified in doing is leaving him to himself, if we do not interfere benevolently by showing interest or concern for him. It is far otherwise if he has infringed the rules necessary for the protection of his fellow creatures, individually or collectively. The evil consequences of his acts do not then fall on himself, but on others; and society, as the protector of all its members, must retaliate on him, must inflict pain on him for the express purpose of punishment, and must take care that it is sufficiently severe. In the one case, he is an offender at our bar, and we are called on not only to sit in judgment on him, but, in one shape or another, to execute our own sentence; in the other case, it is not our part to inflict any suffering on him, except what may incidentally follow from our using the same liberty in the regulation of our own affairs which we allow to him in his.

The distinction here pointed out between the part of a person's life which concerns only himself and that which concerns others, many

persons will refuse to admit.[4] How (it may be asked) can any part of
the conduct of a member of society be a matter of indifference to the
other members? No person is an entirely isolated being; it is impossible for a person to do anything seriously or permanently hurtful to
himself without mischief reaching at least to his near connections, and
often far beyond them. If he injures his property, he does harm to
those who directly or indirectly derived support from it, and usually
diminishes, by a greater or less amount, the general resources of the
community. If he deteriorates his bodily or mental faculties, he not
only brings evil upon all who depended on him for any portion of their
happiness, but disqualifies himself for rendering the services which he
owes to his fellow creatures generally, [and] perhaps becomes a burden
on their affection or benevolence; and if such conduct were very frequent, hardly any offense that is committed would detract more from
the general sum of good. Finally, if by his vices or follies a person does
no direct harm to others, he is nevertheless (it may be said) injurious
by his example, and ought to be compelled to control himself for the
sake of those whom the sight or knowledge of his conduct might corrupt or mislead.

And even (it will be added) if the consequences of misconduct could
be confined to the vicious or thoughtless individual, ought society to
abandon to their own guidance those who are manifestly unfit for it? If
protection against themselves is confessedly due to children and persons
under age, is not society equally bound to afford it to persons of mature
years who are equally incapable of self-government? If gambling, or
drunkenness, or incontinence, or idleness, or uncleanliness are as injurious to happiness, and as great a hindrance to improvement, as many or
most of the acts prohibited by law, why (it may be asked) should not law,
so far as is consistent with practicability and social convenience,
endeavor to repress these also? And as a supplement to the unavoidable
imperfections of law, ought not opinion at least to organize a powerful
police against these vices, and visit rigidly with social penalties those
who are known to practice them? There is no question here (it may be
said) about restricting individuality, or impeding the trial of new and
original experiments in living. The only things it is sought to prevent are
things which have been tried and condemned from the beginning of the
world until now—things which experience has shown not to be useful or
suitable to any person's individuality. There must be some length of time
and amount of experience after which a moral or prudential truth may
be regarded as established; and it is merely desired to prevent generation

after generation from falling over the same precipice which has been fatal to their predecessors.

I fully admit that the mischief which a person does to himself may seriously affect, both through their sympathies and their interests, those nearly connected with him and, in a minor degree, society at large. When, by conduct of this sort, a person is led to violate a distinct and assignable obligation to any other person or persons, the case is taken out of the self-regarding class and becomes amenable to moral disapprobation in the proper sense of the term. If, for example, a man, through intemperance or extravagance, becomes unable to pay his debts, or, having undertaken the moral responsibility of a family, becomes from the same cause incapable of supporting or educating them, he is deservedly reprobated and might be justly punished; but it is for the breach of duty to his family or creditors, not for the extravagence. If the resources which ought to have been devoted to them had been diverted from them for the most prudent investment, the moral culpability would have been the same. George Barnwell murdered his uncle to get money for his mistress, but if he had done it to set himself up in business, he would equally have been hanged.[5] Again, in the frequent case of a man who causes grief to his family by addiction to bad habits, he deserves reproach for his unkindness or ingratitude; but so he may for cultivating habits not in themselves vicious, if they are painful to those with whom he passes his life, or who from personal ties are dependent on him for their comfort. Whoever fails in the consideration generally due to the interests and feelings of others, not being compelled by some more imperative duty, or justified by allowable self-preference, is a subject of moral disapprobation for that failure, but not for the cause of it, nor for the errors, merely personal to himself, which may have remotely led to it. In like manner, when a person disables himself, by conduct purely self-regarding, from the performance of some definite duty incumbent on him to the public, he is guilty of a social offense. No person ought to be punished simply for being drunk; but a soldier or a policeman should be punished for being drunk on duty. Whenever, in short, there is a definite damage, or a definite risk of damage, either to an individual or to the public, the case is taken out of the province of liberty and placed in that of morality or law.   *definite damage vs. contingent injury*

But with regard to the merely contingent or, as it may be called, constructive injury which a person causes to society by conduct which neither violates any specific duty to the public nor occasions perceptible hurt to any assignable individual except himself, the inconvenience is one

which society can afford to bear, for the sake of the greater good of
human freedom. If grown persons are to be punished for not taking
proper care of themselves, I would rather it were for their own sake than
under pretence of preventing them from impairing their capacity of rendering to society benefits which society does not pretend it has a right to
exact. But I cannot consent to argue the point as if society had no means
of bringing its weaker members up to its ordinary standard of rational
conduct, except waiting till they do something irrational, and then punishing them, legally or morally, for it. Society has had absolute power
over them during all the early portion of their existence; it has had the
whole period of childhood and nonage in which to try whether it could
make them capable of rational conduct in life. The existing generation is
master both of the training and the entire circumstances of the generation to come; it cannot indeed make them perfectly wise and good,
because it is itself so lamentably deficient in goodness and wisdom; and
its best efforts are not always, in individual cases, its most successful
ones; but it is perfectly well able to make the rising generation, as a
whole, as good as, and a little better than, itself. If society lets any considerable number of its members grow up mere children, incapable of
being acted on by rational consideration of distant motives, society has
itself to blame for the consequences. Armed not only with all the powers
of education, but with the ascendancy which the authority of a received
opinion always exercises over the minds who are least fitted to judge for
themselves, and aided by the *natural* penalties which cannot be prevented from falling on those who incur the distaste or the contempt of
those who know them—let not society pretend that it needs, besides all
this, the power to issue commands and enforce obedience in the personal
concerns of individuals, in which, on all principles of justice and policy,
the decision ought to rest with those who are to abide the consequences.
Nor is there anything which tends more to discredit and frustrate the better means of influencing conduct than a resort to the worse. If there are
among those whom it is attempted to coerce into prudence or temperance any of the material of which vigorous and independent characters
are made, they will infallibly rebel against the yoke. No such person will
ever feel that others have a right to control him in his concerns, such as
they have to prevent him from injuring them in theirs; and it easily comes
to be considered a mark of spirit and courage to fly in the face of such
usurped authority, and do with ostentation the exact opposite of what it
enjoins, as in the fashion of grossness which succeeded, in the time of
Charles II, to the fanatical moral intolerance of the Puritans.[6] With

respect to what is said of the necessity of protecting society from the bad example set to others by the vicious or the self-indulgent, it is true that bad example may have a pernicious effect, especially the example of doing wrong to others with impunity to the wrongdoer. But we are now speaking of conduct which, while it does no wrong to others, is supposed to do great harm to the agent himself; and I do not see how those who believe this can think otherwise than that the example, on the whole, must be more salutary than hurtful, since, if it displays the misconduct, it displays also the painful or degrading consequences which, if the conduct is justly censured, must be supposed to be in all or most cases attendant on it.

But the strongest of all the arguments against the interference of the public with purely personal conduct is that, when it does interfere, the odds are that it interferes wrongly and in the wrong place. On questions of social morality, of duty to others, the opinion of the public, that is, of an overruling majority, though often wrong, is likely to be still more often right, because on such questions they are only required to judge of their own interests, of the manner in which some mode of conduct, if allowed to be practiced, would affect themselves. But the opinion of a similar majority, imposed as a law on the minority, on questions of self-regarding conduct, is quite as likely to be wrong as right, for in these cases *public opinion* means, at the best, some people's opinion of what is good or bad for other people, while very often it does not even mean that—the public, with the most perfect indifference, passing over the pleasure or convenience of those whose conduct they censure and considering only their own preference. There are many who consider as an injury to themselves any conduct which they have a distaste for, and resent it as an outrage to their feelings; as a religious bigot, when charged with disregarding the religious feelings of others, has been known to retort that they disregard his feelings by persisting in their abominable worship or creed. But there is no parity between the feeling of a person for his own opinion and the feeling of another who is offended at his holding it—no more than between the desire of a thief to take a purse and the desire of the right owner to keep it. And a person's taste is as much his own peculiar concern as his opinion or his purse. It is easy for anyone to imagine an ideal public which leaves the freedom and choice of individuals in all uncertain matters undisturbed and only requires them to abstain from modes of conduct which universal experience has condemned. But where has there been seen a public which set any such limit to its censorship? Or when does the public trouble itself about universal experience? In its interferences with personal conduct it is seldom thinking of anything but the enormity of acting or feeling differently from itself; and this standard of judgment, thinly disguised, is held up to mankind as the dictate of religion and philosophy by nine-tenths of all moralists and speculative writers. These teach that things are right because they are right; because we feel them to be so. They tell us to search in our own minds and hearts for laws of conduct binding on ourselves and on all others. What can the poor public do but apply these instructions and make their own personal feelings of good and evil, if they are tolerably unanimous in them, obligatory on all the world?

The evil here pointed out is not one which exists only in theory; and it may perhaps be expected that I should specify the instances in which the public of this age and country improperly invests its own preferences with the character of moral laws. I am not writing an essay on the aberrations of existing moral feeling. That is too weighty a subject to be discussed parenthetically and by way of illustration. Yet examples are necessary to show that the principle I maintain is of serious and practical moment, and that I am not endeavoring to erect a barrier against imaginary evils. And it is not difficult to show, by abundant instances, that to extend the bounds of what may be called *moral police* until it encroaches on the most unquestionably legitimate liberty of the individual, is one of the most universal of all human propensities.

As a first instance, consider the antipathies which men cherish on no better grounds than that persons whose religious opinions are different from theirs do not practice their religious observances, especially their religious abstinences. To cite a rather trivial example, nothing in the creed or practice of Christians does more to envenom the hatred of Mohammedans[7] against them than the fact of their eating pork. There are few acts which Christians and Europeans regard with more unaffected disgust than Muslims regard this particular mode of satisfying hunger. It is, in the first place, an offense against their religion; but this circumstance by no means explains either the degree or the kind of their repugnance; for wine also is forbidden by their religion, and to partake of it is by all Muslims accounted wrong, but not disgusting. Their aversion to the flesh of the "unclean beast" is, on the contrary, of that peculiar character, resembling an instinctive antipathy, which the idea of uncleanness, when once it thoroughly sinks into the feelings, seems always to excite even in those whose personal habits are anything but scrupulously cleanly, and of which the sentiment of religious impurity, so intense in the Hindus, is a remarkable example. Suppose now that in a people of whom the majority were Muslims, that majority should insist upon not permitting pork to be eaten within the limits of the country. This would be nothing new in Mohammedan countries.* Would it be a legitimate exercise of the moral authority of public opinion? And, if not, why not? The practice is really revolting to such a public. They also sincerely think that it is forbidden and abhorred by the Deity. Neither could the prohibition be censured as religious persecution. It might be religious in its origin, but it would not be persecution for religion, since nobody's religion makes it a duty to eat pork. The only tenable ground of condemnation would be that with the personal tastes and self-regarding concerns of individuals the public has no business to interfere.

To come somewhat nearer home: the majority of Spaniards consider it a gross impiety, offensive in the highest degree to the Supreme Being, to worship him in any other manner than the Roman Catholic; and no other public worship is lawful on Spanish soil. The people of all southern Europe look upon a married clergy as not only irreligious, but unchaste, indecent, gross, disgusting. What do Protestants think of these perfectly sincere feelings, and of the attempt to enforce them against non-Catholics? Yet, if mankind are justified in interfering with each other's liberty in things which do not concern the interests of others, on what principle is it possible consistently to exclude these cases? Or who can blame people for desiring to suppress what they regard as a scandal in the sight of God and man? No stronger case can be shown for prohibiting anything which is regarded as a personal immorality than is made out for suppressing these practices in the eyes of those who regard them as impieties; and unless we are willing to adopt the logic of persecutors, and to say that we may persecute others because we are right, and that

---

* The case of the Bombay Parsees is a curious instance in point. [Editor: "Bombay Parsees" refers to the Zoroastrian Persians who fled to India after the Islamic conquest of Persia to escape Muslim persecution. Zoroastrianism, the oldest of the world's revealed religions, takes its name from the prophet Zoroaster, or Zarathustra (c. 1200-1000 B.C.E.).] When this industrious and enterprising tribe, the descendants of the Persian fire-worshippers, flying from their native country before the Caliphs, arrived in Western India, they were admitted to toleration by the Hindu sovereigns, on condition of not eating beef. When those regions afterwards fell under the dominion of Mohammedan conquerors, the Parsees obtained from them a continuance of indulgence, on condition of refraining from pork. What was at first obedience to authority became a second nature, and the Parsees to this day abstain both from beef and pork. Though not required by their religion, the double abstinence has had time to grow into a custom of their tribe; and custom, in the East, is a religion.

they must not persecute us because they are wrong, we must beware of admitting a principle of which we should resent as a gross injustice the application to ourselves.

The preceding instances may be objected to, although unreasonably, as drawn from contingencies impossible among us—opinion, in this country, not being likely to enforce abstinence from meats, or to interfere with people for worshipping, and for either marrying or not marrying, according to their creed or inclination. The next example, however, shall be taken from an interference with liberty which we have by no means passed all danger of. Wherever the Puritans have been sufficiently powerful, as in New England, and in Great Britain at the time of the Commonwealth, they have endeavored, with considerable success, to put down all public, and nearly all private, amusements: especially music, dancing, public games, or other assemblages for purposes of diversion, and the theater. There are still in this country large bodies of persons by whose notions of morality and religion these recreations are condemned; and those persons belonging chiefly to the middle class, who are the ascendant power in the present social and political condition of the kingdom, it is by no means impossible that persons of these sentiments may at some time or other command a majority in Parliament. How will the remaining portion of the community like to have the amusements that shall be permitted to them regulated by the religious and moral sentiments of the stricter Calvinists and Methodists?[8] Would they not, with considerable peremptoriness, desire these intrusively pious members of society to mind their own business? This is precisely what should be said to every government and every public who have the pretension that no person shall enjoy any pleasure which they think wrong. But if the principle of the pretension is admitted, no one can reasonably object to its being acted on in the sense of the majority, or other preponderating power in the country; and all persons must be ready to conform to the idea of a Christian commonwealth as understood by the early settlers in New England if a religious profession similar to theirs should ever succeed in regaining its lost ground, as religions supposed to be declining have so often been known to do.

To imagine another contingency perhaps more likely to be realized than the one last mentioned. There is confessedly a strong tendency in the modern world towards a democratic constitution of society, accompanied or not by popular political institutions. It is affirmed that in the country where this tendency is most completely realized—where both society and the government are most democratic: the United States—the feeling of the majority, to whom any appearance of a more showy or costly style of living than they can hope to rival is disagreeable, operates as a tolerably effectual sumptuary law,[9] and that in many parts of the Union it is really difficult for a person possessing a very large income to find any mode of spending it which will not incur popular disapprobation. Though such statements as these are doubtless much exaggerated as a representation of existing facts, the state of things they describe is not only a conceivable and possible, but a probable result of democratic feeling combined with the notion that the public has a right to a veto on the manner in which individuals shall spend their incomes. We have only further to suppose a considerable diffusion of socialist opinions, and it may become infamous in the eyes of the majority to possess more property than some very small amount, or any income not earned by manual labor. Opinions similar in principle to these already prevail widely among the artisan class and weigh oppressively on those who are amenable to the opinion chiefly of that class, namely, its own members. It is known that the bad workmen who form the majority of the operatives in many branches of industry are decidedly of [the] opinion that bad workmen ought to receive the same wages as good, and that no one ought to be allowed, through piecework or otherwise, to earn by superior skill or industry more than others can without it. And they employ a moral police, which occasionally becomes a physical one, to deter skillful workmen from receiving, and employers from giving, a larger remuneration for a more useful service. If the public have any jurisdiction over private concerns, I cannot see that these people are in fault, or that any individual's particular public can be blamed for asserting the same authority over his individual conduct which the general public asserts over people in general.

But, without dwelling upon supposititious[10] cases, there are, in our own day, gross usurpations upon the liberty of private life actually practiced, and still greater ones threatened with some expectation of success, and opinions propounded* which assert an unlimited right in the public not only to prohibit by law everything which it thinks wrong, but, in order to get at what it thinks wrong, to prohibit any number of things which it admits to be innocent.

Under the name of preventing intemperance, the people of one English colony, and of nearly half the United States, have been interdicted by law

---

* propounded—proposed (1859a, 1859b).

from making any use whatever of fermented drinks, except for medical purposes—for prohibition of their sale is in fact, as it is intended to be, prohibition of their use. And though the impracticability of executing the law has caused its repeal in several of the States which had adopted it, including the one from which it derives its name,[11] an attempt has notwithstanding been commenced, and is prosecuted with considerable zeal by many of the professed philanthropists, to agitate for a similar law in this country. The association, or "Alliance" as it terms itself, which has been formed for this purpose, has acquired some notoriety through the publicity given to a correspondence between its Secretary and one of the very few English public men who hold that a politician's opinions ought to be founded on principles.[12] Lord Stanley's share in this correspondence is calculated to strengthen the hopes already built on him by those who know how rare such qualities as are manifested in some of his public appearances unhappily are among those who figure in political life. The organ of the Alliance, who would "deeply deplore the recognition of any principle which could be wrested to justify bigotry and persecution," undertakes to point out the "broad and impassable barrier" which divides such principles from those of the association. "All matters relating to thought, opinion, conscience, appear to me," he says, "to be without the sphere of legislation; all pertaining to social act, habit, relation, subject only to a discretionary power vested in the State itself, and not in the individual, to be within it." No mention is made of a third class, different from either of these, viz., acts and habits which are not social, but individual; although it is to this class, surely, that the act of drinking fermented liquors belongs. Selling fermented liquors, however, is trading, and trading is a social act. But the infringement complained of is not on the liberty of the seller, but on that of the buyer and consumer; since the State might just as well forbid him to drink wine as purposely make it impossible for him to obtain it. The Secretary, however, says, "I claim, as a citizen, a right to legislate whenever my social rights are invaded by the social act of another." And now for the definition of these "social rights." "If anything invades my social rights, certainly the traffic in strong drink does. It destroys my primary right of security by constantly creating and stimulating social disorder. It invades my right of equality by deriving a profit from the creation of a misery I am taxed to support. It impedes my right to free moral and intellectual development by surrounding my path with dangers and by weakening and demoralizing society, from which I have a right to claim mutual aid and intercourse." A theory of "social rights" the like of which probably never before found its way into distinct language: being nothing short of this—that it is the absolute social right of every individual that every other individual shall act in every respect exactly as he ought; that whosoever fails of that in the smallest particular violates my social right and entitles me to demand from the legislature the removal of the grievance. So monstrous a principle is far more dangerous than any single interference with liberty; there is no violation of liberty which it would not justify; it acknowledges no right to any freedom whatever, except perhaps to that of holding opinions in secret, without ever disclosing them; for the moment an opinion which I consider noxious passes anyone's lips, it invades all the "social rights" attributed to me by the Alliance. The doctrine ascribes to all mankind a vested interest in each other's moral, intellectual, and even physical perfection, to be defined by each claimant according to his own standard.

Another important example of illegitimate interference with the rightful liberty of the individual, not simply threatened, but long since carried into triumphant effect, is Sabbatarian legislation.[13] Without doubt, abstinence on one day in the week, so far as the exigencies of life permit, from the usual daily occupation, though in no respect religiously binding on any except Jews, is a highly beneficial custom. And inasmuch as this custom cannot be observed without a general consent to that effect among the industrious classes, therefore, in so far as some persons by working may impose the same necessity on others, it may be allowable and right that the law should guarantee to each the observance by others of the custom, by suspending the greater operations of industry on a particular day. But this justification, grounded on the direct interest which others have in each individual's observance of the practice, does not apply to the self-chosen occupations in which a person may think fit to employ his leisure, nor does it hold good, in the smallest degree, for legal restrictions on amusements. It is true that the amusement of some is the day's work of others; but the pleasure, not to say the useful recreation, of many is worth the labor of a few, provided the occupation is freely chosen and can be freely resigned. The operatives are perfectly right in thinking that if all worked on Sunday, seven days' work would have to be given for six days' wages; but so long as the great mass of employments are suspended, the small number who for the enjoyment of others must still work obtain a proportional increase of earnings; and they are not obliged to follow those occupations if they prefer leisure to emolument.[14] If a further remedy is sought, it might be found in the establishment by custom of a holiday on some other day of the week for those particular classes of persons. The only ground, therefore, on which restrictions on Sunday amusements can be defended must be that they are religiously wrong; a motive of legislation which never can be too earnestly protested against. "*Deorum injuriæ Diis curæ*".[15] It remains to be proved that society or any of its officers holds a commission from on high to avenge any supposed offense to Omnipotence which is not also a wrong to our fellow creatures. The notion that it is one man's duty that another should be religious was the foundation of all the religious persecutions ever perpetrated, and, if admitted, would fully justify them. Though the feeling which breaks out in the repeated attempts to stop railway traveling on Sunday, in the resistance to the opening of museums, and the like, has not the cruelty of the old persecutors, the state of mind indicated by it is fundamentally the same. It is a determination not to tolerate others in doing what is permitted by their religion, because it is not permitted by the persecutor's religion. It is a belief that God not only abominates the act of the misbeliever, but will not hold us guiltless if we leave him unmolested.

I cannot refrain from adding to these examples of the little account commonly made of human liberty, the language of downright persecution which breaks out from the press of this country whenever it feels called on to notice the remarkable phenomenon of Mormonism.[16] Much might be said on the unexpected and instructive fact that an alleged new revelation and a religion founded on it—the product of palpable imposture,[17] not even supported by the *prestige* of extraordinary qualities in its founder—is believed by hundreds of thousands, and has been made the foundation of a society in the age of newspapers, railways, and the electric telegraph. What here concerns us is that this religion, like other and better religions, has its martyrs; that its prophet and founder was, for his teaching, put to death by a mob; that others of its adherents lost their lives by the same lawless violence; that they were forcibly expelled, in a body, from the country in which they first grew up; while, now that they have been chased into a solitary recess in the midst of a desert, many in this country openly declare that it would be right (only that it is not convenient) to send an expedition against them and compel them by force to conform to the opinions of other people. The article of the Mormonite doctrine which is the chief provocative to the antipathy which thus breaks through the ordinary restraints of religious tolerance is its sanction of polygamy; which, though permitted to Mohammedans, and Hindus, and Chinese, seems to excite unquenchable animosity when practiced by persons who speak English and profess to be a kind of

Christians. No one has a deeper disapprobation than I have of this Mormon institution; both for other reasons and because, far from being in any way countenanced by the principle of liberty, it is a direct infraction of that principle, being a mere riveting of the chains of one-half of the community, and an emancipation of the other from reciprocity of obligation towards them. Still, it must be remembered that this relation is as much voluntary on the part of the women concerned in it, and who may be deemed the sufferers by it, as is the case with any other form of the marriage institution; and however surprising this fact may appear, it has its explanation in the common ideas and customs of the world, which teaching women to think marriage the one thing needful, make it intelligible that many a woman should prefer being one of several wives to not being a wife at all. Other countries are not asked to recognize such unions, or release any portion of their inhabitants from their own laws on the score of Mormonite opinions. But when the dissentients have conceded to the hostile sentiments of others far more than could justly be demanded; when they have left the countries to which their doctrines were unacceptable and established themselves in a remote corner of the earth, which they have been the first to render habitable to human beings, it is difficult to see on what principles but those of tyranny they can be prevented from living there under what laws they please, provided they commit no aggression on other nations and allow perfect freedom of departure to those who are dissatisfied with their ways. A recent writer, in some respects of considerable merit, proposes (to use his own words) not a crusade, but a *civilizade*, against this polygamous community, to put an end to what seems to him a retrograde step in civilization. It also appears so to me, but I am not aware that any community has a right to force another to be civilized. So long as the sufferers by the bad law do not invoke assistance from other communities, I cannot admit that persons entirely unconnected with them ought to step in and require that a condition of things with which all who are directly interested appear to be satisfied should be put an end to because it is a scandal to persons some thousands of miles distant who have no part or concern in it. Let them send missionaries, if they please, to preach against it; and let them, by any fair means (of which silencing the teachers is not one), oppose the progress of similar doctrines among their own people. If civilization has got the better of barbarism when barbarism had the world to itself, it is too much to profess to be afraid lest barbarism, after having been fairly got under, should revive and conquer civilization. A civilization that can thus succumb to its vanquished enemy must first have

146 John Stuart Mill: On Liberty

become so degenerate that neither its appointed priests and teachers, nor anybody else, has the capacity, or will take the trouble, to stand up for it. If this is so, the sooner such a civilization receives notice to quit, the better. It can only go on from bad to worse until destroyed and regenerated (like the Western Empire) by energetic barbarians.[18]

CHAPTER V

Applications

THE principles asserted in these pages must be more generally admitted as the basis for discussion of details before a consistent application of them to all the various departments of government and morals can be attempted with any prospect of advantage. The few observations I propose to make on questions of detail are designed to illustrate the principles rather than to follow them out to their consequences. I offer not so much applications as specimens of application, which may serve to bring into greater clearness the meaning and limits of the two maxims which together form the entire doctrine of this essay, and to assist the judgment in holding the balance between them in the cases where it appears doubtful which of them is applicable to the case.

The maxims are, first, that the individual is not accountable to society for his actions in so far as these concern the interests of no person but himself. Advice, instruction, persuasion, and avoidance by other people, if thought necessary by them for their own good, are the only measures by which society can justifiably express its dislike or disapprobation of his conduct. Secondly, that for such actions as are prejudicial to the interests of others, the individual is accountable and may be subjected either to social or to legal punishment* if society is of [the] opinion that the one or the other is requisite for its protection.

In the first place, it must by no means be supposed, because damage, or probability of damage, to the interests of others can alone justify the interference of society, that therefore it always does justify such interfer-

---

* punishment—punishments (1859a, 1859b).

ence.[1] In many cases, an individual, in pursuing a legitimate object, necessarily and therefore legitimately causes pain or loss to others, or intercepts a good which they had a reasonable hope of obtaining. Such oppositions of interest between individuals often arise from bad social institutions, but are unavoidable while those institutions last; and some would be unavoidable under any institutions. Whoever succeeds in an overcrowded profession or in a competitive examination; whoever is preferred to another in any contest for an object which both desire, reaps benefit from the loss of others, from their wasted exertion and their disappointment. But it is, by common admission, better for the general interest of mankind that persons should pursue their objects undeterred by this sort of consequences. In other words, society admits no right, either legal or moral, in the disappointed competitors to immunity from this kind of suffering, and feels called on to interfere only when means of success have been employed which it is contrary to the general interest to permit—namely, fraud or treachery, and force.

Again, trade is a social act. Whoever undertakes to sell any description of goods to the public does what affects the interest of other persons and of society in general; and thus his conduct, in principle, comes within the jurisdiction of society; accordingly, it was once held to be the duty of governments, in all cases which were considered of importance, to fix prices and regulate the processes of manufacture. But it is now recognized, though not till after a long struggle, that both the cheapness and the good quality of commodities are most effectually provided for by leaving the producers and sellers perfectly free, under the sole check of equal freedom to the buyers for supplying themselves elsewhere. This is the so-called doctrine of free trade,[2] which rests on grounds different from, though equally solid with, the principle of individual liberty asserted in this essay. Restrictions on trade, or on production for purposes of trade, are indeed restraints; and all restraint, *quâ* restraint, is an evil; but the restraints in question affect only that part of conduct which society is competent to restrain, and are wrong solely because they do not really produce the results which it is desired to produce by them. As the principle of individual liberty is not involved in the doctrine of free trade, so neither is it in most of the questions which arise respecting the limits of that doctrine, as, for example, what amount of public control is admissible for the prevention of fraud by adulteration; [or] how far sanitary precautions, or arrangements to protect work-people employed in dangerous occupations, should be enforced on employers. Such questions involve considerations of liberty only in so far as leaving people to themselves is always better, *cæteris paribus*,[3] than controlling them; but that they may be legitimately controlled for these ends is in principle undeniable. On the other hand, there are questions relating to interference with trade which are essentially questions of liberty, such as the Maine Law, already touched upon;[4] the prohibition of the importation of opium into China;[5] the restriction of the sale of poisons—all cases, in short, where the object of the interference is to make it impossible or difficult to obtain a particular commodity. These interferences are objectionable, not as infringements on the liberty of the producer or seller, but on that of the buyer.

One of these examples, that of the sale of poisons, opens a new question: the proper limits of what may be called the functions of police—how far liberty may legitimately be invaded for the prevention of crime, or of accident. It is one of the undisputed functions of government to take precautions against crime before it has been committed, as well as to detect and punish it afterwards. The preventive function of government, however, is far more liable to be abused, to the prejudice of liberty, than the punitory[6] function; for there is hardly any part of the legitimate freedom of action of a human being which would not admit of being represented, and fairly too, as increasing the facilities for some form or other of delinquency. Nevertheless, if a public authority, or even a private person, sees anyone evidently preparing to commit a crime, they are not bound to look on inactive until the crime is committed, but may interfere to prevent it. If poisons were never bought or used for any purpose except the commission of murder, it would be right to prohibit their manufacture and sale. They may, however, be wanted not only for innocent but for useful purposes, and restrictions cannot be imposed in the one case without operating in the other. Again, it is a proper office of public authority to guard against accidents. If either a public officer or anyone else saw a person attempting to cross a bridge which had been ascertained to be unsafe, and there were no time to warn him of his danger, they might seize him and turn him back without any real infringement of his liberty; for liberty consists in doing what one desires, and he does not desire to fall into the river. Nevertheless, when there is not a certainty, but only a danger of mischief, no one but the person himself can judge of the sufficiency of the motive which may prompt him to incur the risk; in this case, therefore, (unless he is a child, or delirious, or in some state of excitement or absorption incompatible with the full use of the reflecting faculty) he ought, I conceive, to be only warned of the danger, not forcibly prevented from exposing himself to it. Similar considerations, applied to such a question as the

sale of poisons, may enable us to decide which among the possible modes
of regulation are or are not contrary to principle. Such a precaution, for
example, as that of labeling the drug with some word expressive of its
dangerous character may be enforced without violation of liberty: the
buyer cannot wish not to know that the thing he possesses has poisonous
qualities. But to require in all cases the certificate of a medical practitioner
would make it sometimes impossible, always expensive, to obtain the
article for legitimate uses. The only mode apparent to me in which difficulties may be thrown in the way of crime committed through this means,
without any infringement worth taking into account upon the liberty of
those who desire the poisonous substance for other purposes, consists in
providing what, in the apt language of Bentham, is called "preappointed
evidence."[7] This provision is familiar to everyone in the case of contracts.
It is usual and right that the law, when a contract is entered into, should
require as the condition of its enforcing performance that certain formali-
ties should be observed, such as signatures, attestation of witnesses, and
the like, in order that in case of subsequent dispute there may be evidence
to prove that the contract was really entered into, and that there was
nothing in the circumstances to render it legally invalid—the effect being
to throw great obstacles in the way of fictitious contracts or contracts
made in circumstances which, if known, would destroy their validity. Precautions of a similar nature might be enforced in the sale of articles
adapted to be instruments of crime. The seller, for example, might be
required to enter in a register the exact time of the transaction, the name
and address of the buyer, the precise quality and quantity sold; to ask the
purpose for which it was wanted, and record the answer he received.
When there was no medical prescription, the presence of some third person might be required to bring home the fact to the purchaser, in case
there should afterwards be reason to believe that the article had been
applied to criminal purposes. Such regulations would in general be no
material impediment to obtaining the article, but a very considerable one
to making an improper use of it without detection.

The right inherent in society to ward off crimes against itself by
antecedent precautions suggests the obvious limitations to the maxim
that purely self-regarding misconduct cannot properly be meddled with
in the way of prevention or punishment. Drunkenness, for example, in
ordinary cases, is not a fit subject for legislative interference; but I should
deem it perfectly legitimate that a person who had once been convicted
of any act of violence to others under the influence of drink should be
placed under a special legal restriction, personal to himself; that if he

were afterwards found drunk, he should be liable to a penalty, and that if when in that state he committed another offense, the punishment to which he would be liable for that other offense should be increased in severity. The making himself drunk, in a person whom drunkenness excites to do harm to others, is a crime against others. So, again, idleness, except in a person receiving support from the public, or except when it constitutes a breach of contract, cannot without tyranny be made a subject of legal punishment; but if, either from idleness or from any other avoidable cause, a man fails to perform his legal duties to others, as for instance to support his children, it is no tyranny to force him to fulfill that obligation by compulsory labor if no other means are available.

Again, there are many acts which, being directly injurious only to the agents themselves, ought not to be legally interdicted, but which, if done publicly, are a violation of good manners and, coming thus within the category of offenses against others, may rightfully be prohibited. Of this kind are offenses against decency—on which it is unnecessary to dwell, the rather as they are only connected indirectly with our subject, the objection to publicity being equally strong in the case of many actions not in themselves condemnable, nor supposed to be so.

There is another question to which an answer must be found, consistent with the principles which have been laid down. In cases of personal conduct supposed to be blamable, but which respect for liberty precludes society from preventing or punishing because the evil directly resulting falls wholly on the agent; what the agent is free to do, ought other persons to be equally free to counsel or instigate? This question is not free from difficulty. The case of a person who solicits another to do an act is not strictly a case of self-regarding conduct. To give advice or offer inducements to anyone is a social act, and may, therefore, like actions in general which affect others, be supposed amenable to social control. But a little reflection corrects the first impression, by showing that if the case is not strictly within the definition of individual liberty, yet the reasons on which the principle of individual liberty is grounded are applicable to it. If people must be allowed, in whatever concerns only themselves, to act as seems best to themselves at their own peril, they must equally be free to consult with one another about what is fit to be so done; to exchange opinions, and give and receive suggestions. Whatever it is permitted to do, it must be permitted to advise to do. The question is doubtful only when the instigator derives a personal benefit from his advice; when he makes it his occupation, for subsistence or pecuniary gain, to promote what society and the state consider to be an evil. Then, indeed,

John Stuart Mill: On Liberty

a new element of complication is introduced—namely, the existence of classes of persons with an interest opposed to what is considered as the public weal,[8] and whose mode of living is grounded on the counteraction of it. Ought this to be interfered with, or not? Fornication, for example, must be tolerated, and so must gambling; but should a person be free to be a pimp, or to keep a gambling-house? The case is one of those which lie on the exact boundary line between two principles, and it is not at once apparent to which of the two it properly belongs. There are arguments on both sides. On the side of toleration it may be said that the fact of following anything as an occupation, and living or profiting by the practice of it, cannot make that criminal which would otherwise be admissible; that the act should either be consistently permitted or consistently prohibited; that if the principles which we have up till now defended are true, society has no business, *as* society, to decide anything to be wrong which concerns only the individual; that it cannot go beyond dissuasion, and that one person should be as free to persuade, as another to dissuade. In opposition to this it may be contended that, although the public, or the state, are not warranted in authoritatively deciding, for purposes of repression or punishment, that such or such conduct affecting only the interests of the individual is good or bad, they are fully justified in assuming, if they regard it as bad, that its being so or not is at least a disputable question: that, this being supposed, they cannot be acting wrongly in endeavoring to exclude the influence of solicitations which are not disinterested, of instigators who cannot possibly be impartial—who have a direct personal interest on one side, and that side the one which the state believes to be wrong, and who confessedly promote it for personal objects only. There can surely, it may be urged, be nothing lost, no sacrifice of good, by so ordering matters that persons shall make their election, either wisely or foolishly, on their own prompting, as free as possible from the arts of persons who stimulate their inclinations for interested purposes of their own. Thus (it may be said), though the statutes respecting unlawful games are utterly indefensible— though all persons should be free to gamble in their own or each other's houses, or in any place of meeting established by their own subscriptions and open only to the members and their visitors—yet public gambling-houses should not be permitted. It is true that the prohibition is never effectual, and that, whatever amount of tyrannical power may be* given

---

* may be—is (1859a, 1859b).

t is legal to have sex
so shouldn't you be able to make money
having sex
Applications   153

to the police, gambling-houses can always be maintained under other pretenses; but they may be compelled to conduct their operations with a certain degree of secrecy and mystery, so that nobody knows anything about them but those who seek them; and more than this society ought not to aim at. There is considerable force in these arguments. I* will not venture to decide whether they are sufficient to justify the moral anomaly of punishing the accessory when the principal is (and must be) allowed to go free—of fining or imprisoning the procurer, but not the fornicator; the gambling-house keeper, but not the gambler. Still less ought the common operations of buying and selling to be interfered with on analogous grounds. Almost every article which is bought and sold may be used in excess, and the sellers have a pecuniary interest in encouraging that excess; but no argument can be founded on this in favor, for instance, of the Maine Law; because the class of dealers in strong drinks, though interested in their abuse, are indispensably required for the sake of their legitimate use. The interest, however, of these dealers in promoting intemperance is a real evil, and justifies the state in imposing restrictions and requiring guarantees which, but for that justification, would be infringements of legitimate liberty.

A further question is whether the state, while it permits, should never-theless indirectly discourage conduct which it deems contrary to the best interests of the agent; whether, for example, it should take measures to render the means of drunkenness more costly, or add to the difficulty of procuring them by limiting the number of the places of sale. On this, as on most other practical questions, many distinctions require to be made. To tax stimulants for the sole purpose of making them more difficult to be obtained is a measure differing only in degree from their entire prohi-bition, and would be justifiable only if that were justifiable. Every increase of cost is a prohibition to those whose means do not come up to the augmented price; and to those who do, it is a penalty laid on them for gratifying a particular taste. Their choice of pleasures, and their mode of expending their income, after satisfying their legal and moral obligations to the state and to individuals, are their own concern and must rest with their own judgment. These considerations may seem at first sight to con-demn the selection of stimulants as special subjects of taxation for pur-poses of revenue. But it must be remembered that taxation for fiscal purposes is absolutely inevitable; that in most countries it is necessary

---

* arguments. I—arguments; I (1859a, 1859b).

that a considerable part of that taxation should be indirect; that the state, therefore, cannot help imposing penalties, which to some persons may be prohibitory, on the use of some articles of consumption. It is hence the duty of the state to consider, in the imposition of taxes, what commodities the consumers can best spare; and *à fortiori,*[9] to select in preference those of which it deems the use, beyond a very moderate quantity, to be positively injurious. Taxation, therefore, of stimulants up to the point which produces the largest amount of revenue (supposing that the state needs all the revenue which it yields) is not only admissible, but to be approved of.

The question of making the sale of these commodities a more or less exclusive privilege must be answered differently, according to the purposes to which the restriction is intended to be subservient. All places of public resort require the restraint of a police, and places of this kind peculiarly, because offenses against society are especially apt to originate there. It is, therefore, fit to confine the power of selling these commodities (at least for consumption on the spot) to persons of known or vouched-for respectability of conduct; to make such regulations respecting hours of opening and closing as may be requisite for public surveillance, and to withdraw the license if breaches of the peace repeatedly take place through the connivance or incapacity of the keeper of the house, or if it becomes a rendezvous for concocting and preparing offenses against the law. Any further restriction I do not conceive to be, in principle, justifiable. The limitation in number, for instance, of beer and spirit houses, for the express purpose of rendering them more difficult of access and diminishing the occasions of temptation, not only exposes all to an inconvenience because there are some by whom the facility would be abused, but is suited only to a state of society in which the laboring classes are avowedly treated as children or savages, and placed under an education of restraint, to fit them for future admission to the privileges of freedom. This is not the principle on which the laboring classes are professedly governed in any free country; and no person who sets due value on freedom will give his adhesion to their being so governed, unless after all efforts have been exhausted to educate them for freedom and govern them as freemen, and it has been definitively proved that they can only be governed as children. The bare statement of the alternative shows the absurdity of supposing that such efforts have been made in any case which needs be considered here. It is only because the institutions of this country are a mass of inconsistencies that things find admittance into our practice which belong to the system of despotic, or what is called paternal, government, while the general freedom of our institutions precludes the exercise of the amount of control necessary to render the restraint of any real efficacy as a moral education.

It was pointed out in an early part of this essay that the liberty of the individual, in things wherein the individual is alone concerned, implies a corresponding liberty in any number of individuals to regulate by mutual agreement such things as regard them jointly, and regard no persons but themselves. This question presents no difficulty so long as the will of all the persons implicated remains unaltered; but since that will may change, it is often necessary, even in things in which they alone are concerned, that they should enter into engagements with one another; and when they do, it is fit, as a general rule, that those engagements should be kept. Yet, in the laws, probably, of every country, this general rule has some exceptions. Not only persons are not held to engagements which violate the rights of third parties, but it is sometimes considered a sufficient reason for releasing them from an engagement that it is injurious to themselves. In this and most other civilized countries, for example, an engagement by which a person should sell himself, or allow himself to be sold, as a slave, would be null and void, neither enforced by law nor by opinion. The ground for thus limiting his power of voluntarily disposing of his own lot in life is apparent, and is very clearly seen in this extreme case. The reason for not interfering, unless for the sake of others, with a person's voluntary acts is consideration for his liberty. His voluntary choice is evidence that what he so chooses is desirable, or at the least endurable, to him, and his good is on the whole best provided for by allowing him to take his own means of pursuing it. But by selling himself for a slave, he abdicates his liberty; he foregoes any future use of it beyond that single act. He therefore defeats, in his own case, the very purpose which is the justification of allowing him to dispose of himself. He is no longer free, but is from then on in a position which has no longer the presumption in its favor that would be afforded by his voluntarily remaining in it. The principle of freedom cannot require that he should be free not to be free. It is not freedom to be allowed to alienate his freedom. These reasons, the force of which is so conspicuous in this peculiar case, are evidently of far wider application; yet a limit is everywhere set to them by the necessities of life, which continually require, not indeed that we should resign our freedom, but that we should consent to this and the other limitation of it. The principle, however, which demands uncontrolled freedom of action in all that concerns only the agents themselves, requires that those who have become bound to one another, in things which concern no third party, should be able to release one another from the engagement; and even without such voluntary release, there are perhaps no contracts or engagements, except those that relate to money or money's worth, of which one can venture to say that there ought to be no liberty whatever of retraction. Baron Wilhelm von Humboldt, in the excellent essay from which I have already quoted,[10] states it as his conviction that engagements which involve personal relations or services should never be legally binding beyond a limited duration of time; and that the most important of these engagements, marriage, having the peculiarity that its objects are frustrated unless the feelings of both the parties are in harmony with it, should require nothing more than the declared will of either party to dissolve it. This subject is too important, and too complicated, to be discussed in a parenthesis, and I touch on it only so far as is necessary for purposes of illustration. If the conciseness and generality of Baron Humboldt's dissertation had not obliged him in this instance to content himself with enunciating his conclusion without discussing the premises, he would doubtless have recognized that the question cannot be decided on grounds so simple as those to which he confines himself. When a person, either by express promise or by conduct, has encouraged another to rely upon his continuing to act in a certain way—to build expectations and calculations, and stake any part of his plan of life upon that supposition—a new series of moral obligations arises on his part towards that person, which may possibly be overruled, but cannot be ignored. And again, if the relation between two contracting parties has been followed by consequences to others; if it has placed third parties in any peculiar position, or, as in the case of marriage, has even called third parties into existence, obligations arise on the part of both the contracting parties towards those third persons, the fulfillment of which, or at all events the mode of fulfillment, must be greatly affected by the continuance or disruption of the relation between the original parties to the contract. It does not follow, nor can I admit, that these obligations extend to requiring the fulfillment of the contract at all costs to the happiness of the reluctant party; but they are a necessary element in the question; and, even if, as von Humboldt maintains, they ought to make no difference in the *legal* freedom of the parties to release themselves from the engagement (and I also hold that they ought not to make *much* difference), they necessarily make a great difference in the *moral* freedom. A person is bound to take all these circumstances into account before resolving on a step which may affect such important interests of others; and if he does not allow proper weight to those interests, he is morally responsible for the wrong. I have made these obvious remarks for the better illustration of the general principle of liberty, and not because they are at all needed on the particular question, which, on the contrary, is usually discussed as if the interest of children was everything, and that of grown persons nothing.

I have already observed that, owing to the absence of any recognized general principles, liberty is often granted where it should be withheld, as well as withheld where it should be granted; and one of the cases in which, in the modern European world, the sentiment of liberty is the strongest, is a case where, in my view, it is altogether misplaced. A person should be free to do as he likes in his own concerns, but he ought not to be free to do as he likes in acting for another, under the pretext that the affairs of the other* are his own affairs. The state, while it respects the liberty of each in what specially regards himself, is bound to maintain a vigilant control over his exercise of any power which it allows him to possess over others. This obligation is almost entirely disregarded in the case of the family relations—a case, in its direct influence on human happiness, more important than all the others taken together. The almost despotic power of husbands over wives needs not be enlarged upon here, because nothing more is needed for the complete removal of the evil than that wives should have the same rights, and should receive the protection of law in the same manner, as all other persons; and because, on this subject, the defenders of established injustice do not avail themselves of the plea of liberty but stand forth openly as the champions of power. It is in the case of children that misapplied notions of liberty are a real obstacle to the fulfillment by the state of its duties. One would almost think that a man's children were supposed to be literally, and not metaphorically, a part of himself, so jealous is opinion of the smallest interference of law with his absolute and exclusive control over them, more jealous than of almost any interference with his own freedom of action—so much less do the generality of mankind value liberty than power. Consider, for example, the case of education. Is it not almost a self-evident axiom that the state should require and compel the education, up to a certain standard, of every human being who is born its citizen? Yet who is there that is not afraid to recognize and assert this truth? Hardly anyone indeed will deny that it is one of the most sacred duties of the parents (or, as law and usage now stand, the father), after summoning a human being into

* the other—another (1859a, 1859b).

the world, to give to that being an education fitting him to perform his part well in life towards others and towards himself. But while this is unanimously declared to be the father's duty, scarcely anybody, in this country, will bear to hear of obliging him to perform it. Instead of his being required to make any exertion or sacrifice for securing education to the child, it is left to his choice to accept it or not when it is provided gratis! It still remains unrecognized that to bring a child into existence without a fair prospect of being able, not only to provide food for its body, but instruction and training for its mind, is a moral crime, both against the unfortunate offspring and against society; and that if the parent does not fulfill this obligation, the state ought to see it fulfilled at the charge, as far as possible, of the parent. *time to interfere*

Were the duty of enforcing universal education once admitted there would be an end to the difficulties about what the state should teach, and how it should teach, which now convert the subject into a mere battle-field for sects and parties, causing the time and labor which should have been spent in educating to be wasted in quarrelling about education. If the government would make up its mind to *require* for every child a good education, it might save itself the trouble of *providing* one. It might leave to parents to obtain the education where and how they pleased, and content itself with helping to pay the school fees of the poorer classes* of children, and defraying the entire school expenses of those who have no one else to pay for them. The objections which are urged with reason against state education do not apply to the enforcement of education by the state, but to the state's taking upon itself to direct that education, which is a totally different thing. That the whole or any large part of the education of the people should be in state hands, I go as far as any one in deprecating. All that has been said of the importance of individuality of character and diversity in opinions and modes of conduct involves, as of the same unspeakable importance, diversity of education. A general state education is a mere contrivance for molding people to be exactly like one another; and as the mold in which it casts them is that which pleases the predominant power in the government—whether this is a monarch, a priesthood, an aristocracy, or the majority of the existing generation—in proportion as it is efficient and successful, it establishes a despotism over the mind, leading by natural tendency to one over the body. An education established and controlled by the state should only exist, if it exist at

* classes-class (1859a, 1859b).

all, as one among many competing experiments, carried on for the purpose of example and stimulus to keep the others up to a certain standard of excellence. Unless, indeed, when society in general is in so backward a state that it could not or would not provide for itself any proper institutions of education unless the government undertook the task, then, indeed, the government may, as the less of two great evils, take upon itself the business of schools and universities, as it may that of joint stock companies when private enterprise, in a shape fitted for undertaking great works of industry, does not exist in the country. But in general, if the country contains a sufficient number of persons qualified to provide education under government auspices, the same persons would be able and willing to give an equally good education on the voluntary principle, under the assurance of remuneration afforded by a law rendering education compulsory, combined with state aid to those unable to defray the expense.

The instrument for enforcing the law could be no other than public examinations, extending to all children and beginning at an early age. An age might be fixed at which every child must be examined to ascertain if he (or she) is able to read. If a child proves unable, the father, unless he has some sufficient ground of excuse, might be subjected to a moderate fine, to be worked out, if necessary, by his labor, and the child might be put to school at his expense. Once in every year the examination should be renewed, with a gradually extending range of subjects, so as to make the universal acquisition, and what is more, retention, of a certain minimum of general knowledge, virtually compulsory. Beyond that minimum there should be voluntary examinations on all subjects, at which all who come up to a certain standard of proficiency might claim a certificate. To prevent the state from exercising, through these arrangements, an improper influence over opinion, the knowledge required for passing an examination (beyond the merely instrumental parts of knowledge, such as languages and their use) should, even in the higher classes* of examinations, be confined to facts and positive science exclusively. The examinations on religion, politics, or other disputed topics should not turn on the truth or falsehood of opinions, but on the matter of fact that such and such an opinion is held, on such grounds, by such authors, or schools, or churches. Under this system, the rising generation would be no worse off in regard to all disputed truths than they are at present; they

---

* classes-class (1859a, 1859b).

would be brought up either churchmen or dissenters as they now are, the state merely taking care that they should be instructed churchmen or instructed dissenters. There would be nothing to hinder them from being taught religion, if their parents chose, at the same schools where they were taught other things. All attempts by the state to bias the conclusions of its citizens on disputed subjects are evil; but it may very properly offer to ascertain and certify that a person possesses the knowledge requisite to make his conclusions, on any given subject, worth attending to. A student of philosophy would be the better for being able to stand an examination both in Locke and in Kant,[11] whichever of the two he takes up with, or even if with neither: and there is no reasonable objection to examining an atheist in the evidences of Christianity, provided he is not required to profess a belief in them. The examinations, however, in the higher branches of knowledge should, I conceive, be entirely voluntary. It would be giving too dangerous a power to governments were they allowed to exclude anyone from professions, even from the profession of teacher, for alleged deficiency of qualifications; and I think, with Wilhelm von Humboldt, that degrees or other public certificates of scientific or professional acquirements should be given to all who present themselves for examination and stand the test; but that such certificates should confer no advantage over competitors, other than the weight which may be attached to their testimony by public opinion.

It is not in the matter of education only that misplaced notions of liberty prevent moral obligations on the part of parents from being recognized, and legal obligations from being imposed, where there are the strongest grounds for the former always, and in many cases for the latter also. The fact itself, of causing the existence of a human being, is one of the most responsible actions in the range of human life. To undertake this responsibility—to bestow a life which may be either a curse or a blessing—unless the being on whom it is to be bestowed will have at least the ordinary chances of a desirable existence, is a crime against that being. And in a country either over-peopled, or threatened with being so, to produce children, beyond a very small number, with the effect of reducing the reward of labor by their competition is a serious offense against all who live by the remuneration of their labor. The laws which, in many countries on the Continent, forbid marriage unless the parties can show that they have the means of supporting a family do not exceed the legitimate powers of the state; and whether such laws are expedient or not (a question mainly dependent on local circumstances and feelings), they are not objectionable as violations of liberty. Such laws are interferences of the state to prohibit a mischievous act—an act injurious to others, which ought to be a subject of reprobation, and social stigma, even when it is not deemed expedient to superadd legal punishment. Yet the current ideas of liberty, which bend so easily to real infringements of the freedom of the individual, in things which concern only himself, would repel the attempt to put any restraint upon his inclinations when the consequence of their indulgence is a life or lives of wretchedness and depravity to the offspring, with manifold evils to those sufficiently within reach to be in any way affected by their actions. When we compare the strange respect of mankind for liberty with their strange want of respect for it, we might imagine that a man had an indispensable right to do harm to others, and no right at all to please himself without giving pain to any one.

I have reserved for the last place a large class of questions respecting the limits of government interference, which, though closely connected with the subject of this essay, do not, in strictness, belong to it. These are cases in which the reasons against interference do not turn upon the principle of liberty—the question is not about restraining the actions of individuals, but about helping them: it is asked whether the government should do, or cause to be done, something for their benefit, instead of leaving it to be done by themselves, individually, or in voluntary combination.

The objections to government interference, when it is not such as to involve infringement of liberty, may be of three kinds.

The first is when the thing to be done is likely to be better done by individuals than by the government. Speaking generally, there is no one so fit to conduct any business, or to determine how or by whom it shall be conducted, as those who are personally interested in it. This principle condemns the interferences, once so common, of the legislature, or the officers of government, with the ordinary processes of industry. But this part of the subject has been sufficiently enlarged upon by political economists,[12] and is not particularly related to the principles of this essay.

The second objection is more nearly allied to our subject. In many cases, though individuals may not do the particular thing so well, on the average, as the officers of government, it is nevertheless desirable that it should be done by them, rather than by the government, as a means to their own mental education—a mode of strengthening their active faculties, exercising their judgment, and giving them a familiar knowledge of the subjects with which they are thus left to deal. This is a principal, though not the sole, recommendation of jury trial (in cases not political);

of free and popular local and municipal institutions; of the conduct of industrial and philanthropic enterprises by voluntary associations. These are not questions of liberty, and are connected with that subject only by remote tendencies, but they are questions of development. It belongs to a different occasion from the present to dwell on these things as parts of national education, as being, in truth, the peculiar training of a citizen, the practical part of the political education of a free people, taking them out of the narrow circle of personal and family selfishness, and accustoming them to the comprehension of joint interests [and to] the management of joint concerns—habituating them to act from public or semi-public motives, and guide their conduct by aims which unite instead of isolating them from one another. Without these habits and powers, a free constitution can neither be worked nor preserved, as is exemplified by the too-often transitory nature of political freedom in countries where it does not rest upon a sufficient basis of local liberties. The management of purely local business by the localities, and of the great enterprises of industry by the union of those who voluntarily supply the pecuniary means, is further recommended by all the advantages which have been set forth in this essay as belonging to individuality of development and diversity of modes of action. Government operations tend to be everywhere alike. With individuals and voluntary associations, on the contrary, there are varied experiments and endless diversity of experience. What the state can usefully do is to make itself a central depository, and active circulator and diffuser, of the experience resulting from many trials. Its business is to enable each experimentalist to benefit by the experiments of others, instead of tolerating no experiments but its own.

The third and most cogent reason for restricting the interference of government is the great evil of adding unnecessarily to its power. Every function superadded to those already exercised by the government causes its influence over hopes and fears to be more widely diffused, and converts, more and more, the active and ambitious part of the public into hangers-on of the government, or of some party which aims at becoming the government. If the roads, the railways, the banks, the insurance offices, the great joint-stock companies, the universities, and the public charities were all of them branches of the government; if, in addition, the municipal corporations and local boards, with all that now devolves on them, became departments of the central administration; if the employees of all these different enterprises were appointed and paid by the government and looked to the government for every rise in life, not all the freedom of the press and popular constitution of the legislature would make this or any other country free otherwise than in name. And the evil would be greater, the more efficiently and scientifically the administrative machinery was constructed—the more skillful the arrangements for obtaining the best qualified hands and heads with which to work it. In England it has of late been proposed that all the members of the civil service of government should be selected by competitive examination, to obtain for those employments the most intelligent and instructed persons procurable; and much has been said and written for and against this proposal.[13] One of the arguments most insisted on by its opponents is that the occupation of a permanent official servant of the state does not hold out sufficient prospects of emolument and importance to attract the highest talents, which will always be able to find a more inviting career in the professions or in the service of companies and other public bodies. One would not have been surprised if this argument had been used by the friends of the proposition as an answer to its principal difficulty. Coming from the opponents it is strange enough. What is urged as an objection is the safety-valve of the proposed system. If, indeed, all the high talent of the country *could* be drawn into the service of the government, a proposal tending to bring about that result might well inspire uneasiness. If every part of the business of society which required organized concert, or large and comprehensive views, were in the hands of the government, and if government offices were universally filled by the ablest men, all the enlarged culture and practiced intelligence in the country, except the purely speculative, would be concentrated in a numerous bureaucracy, to whom alone the rest of the community would look for all things—the multitude for direction and dictation in all they had to do; the able and aspiring for personal advancement. To be admitted into the ranks of this bureaucracy, and when admitted, to rise therein, would be the sole objects of ambition. Under this regime, not only is the outside public ill-qualified, for want of practical experience, to criticize or check the mode of operation of the bureaucracy, but even if the accidents of despotic or the natural working of popular institutions occasionally raise to the summit a ruler or rulers of reforming inclinations, no reform can be effected which is contrary to the interest of the bureaucracy. Such is the melancholy condition of the Russian empire, as shown* in the accounts of those who have had sufficient opportunity of observation. The Czar himself is powerless against the bureaucratic

---

* as shown—as is shown (1859a, 1859b).

body; he can send any one of them to Siberia, but he cannot govern without them, or against their will. On every decree of his they have a tacit veto, by merely refraining from carrying it into effect. In countries of more advanced civilization and of a more insurrectionary spirit, the public, accustomed to expect everything to be done for them by the state, or at least to do nothing for themselves without asking from the state not only leave to do it, but even how it is to be done, naturally hold the state responsible for all evil which befalls them, and when the evil exceeds their amount of patience, they rise against the government and make what is called a revolution; whereupon somebody else, with or without legitimate authority from the nation, vaults into the seat, issues his orders to the bureaucracy, and everything goes on much as it did before; the bureaucracy being unchanged, and nobody else being capable of taking their place.

A very different spectacle is exhibited among a people accustomed to transact their own business. In France, a large part of the people having been engaged in military service, many of whom have held at least the rank of non-commissioned officers, there are in every popular insurrection several persons competent to take the lead and improvise some tolerable plan of action. What the French are in military affairs, the Americans are in every kind of civil business; let them be left without a government, every body of Americans is able to improvise one and to carry on that or any other public business with a sufficient amount of intelligence, order, and decision. This is what every free people ought to be; and a people capable of this is certain to be free; it will never let itself be enslaved by any man or body of men because these are able to seize and pull the reins of the central administration. No bureaucracy can hope to make such a people as this do or undergo anything that they do not like. But where everything is done through the bureaucracy, nothing to which the bureaucracy is really adverse can be done at all. The constitution of such countries is an organization of the experience and practical ability of the nation into a disciplined body for the purpose of governing the rest; and the more perfect that organization is in itself, the more successful in drawing to itself and educating for itself the persons of greatest capacity from all ranks of the community, the more complete is the bondage of all, the members of the bureaucracy included. For the governors are as much the slaves of their organization and discipline as the governed are of the governors. A Chinese mandarin[14] is as much the tool and creature of a despotism as the humblest cultivator. An individual Jesuit[15] is to the utmost degree of abasement the slave of his order, though the order itself exists for the collective power and importance of its members.

It is not, also, to be forgotten that the absorption of all the principal ability of the country into the governing body is fatal, sooner or later, to the mental activity and progressiveness of the body itself. Banded together as they are—working a system which, like all systems, necessarily proceeds in a great measure by fixed rules—the official body are under the constant temptation of sinking into indolent routine, or, if they now and then desert that mill-horse round,[16] of rushing into some half-examined crudity which has struck the fancy of some leading member of the corps; and the sole check to these closely allied, though seemingly opposite, tendencies, the only stimulus which can keep the ability of the body itself up to a high standard, is liability to the watchful criticism of equal ability outside the body. It is indispensable, therefore, that the means should exist, independently of the government, of forming such ability and furnishing it with the opportunities and experience necessary for a correct judgment of great practical affairs. If we would possess permanently a skillful and efficient body of functionaries—above all, a body able to originate and willing to adopt improvements; if we would not have our bureaucracy degenerate into a pedantocracy,[17] this body must not engross all the occupations which form and cultivate the faculties required for the government of mankind.

To determine the point at which evils, so formidable to human freedom and advancement, begin, or rather at which they begin to predominate over the benefits attending the collective application of the force of society, under its recognized chiefs, for the removal of the obstacles which stand in the way of its well-being; to secure as much of the advantages of centralized power and intelligence as can be had without turning into governmental channels too great a proportion of the general activity—is one of the most difficult and complicated questions in the art of government. It is, in a great measure, a question of detail, in which many and various considerations must be kept in view, and no absolute rule can be laid down. But I believe that the practical principle in which safety resides, the ideal to be kept in view, the standard by which to test all arrangements intended for overcoming the difficulty, may be conveyed in these words: the greatest dissemination of power consistent with efficiency; but the greatest possible centralization of information and diffusion of it from the center. Thus, in municipal administration, there would be, as in the New England States, a very minute division among separate officers, chosen by the localities, of all business which is not better left to the persons directly interested; but besides this, there would be, in each department of local affairs, a central superintendence, forming a branch of the general government. The organ of this superintendence would concentrate, as in a focus, the variety of information and experience derived from the conduct of that branch of public business in all the localities, from everything analogous which is done in foreign countries, and from the general principles of political science. This central organ should have a right to know all that is done, and its special duty should be that of making the knowledge acquired in one place available for others. Emancipated from the petty prejudices and narrow views of a locality by its elevated position and comprehensive sphere of observation, its advice would naturally carry much authority; but its actual power, as a permanent institution, should, I conceive, be limited to compelling the local officers to obey the laws laid down for their guidance. In all things not provided for by general rules, those officers should be left to their own judgment, under responsibility to their constituents. For the violation of rules, they should be responsible to law, and the rules themselves should be laid down by the legislature; the central administrative authority only watching over their execution, and if they were not properly carried into effect, appealing, according to the nature of the case, to the tribunals* to enforce the law, or to the constituencies to dismiss the functionaries who had not executed it according to its spirit. Such, in its general conception, is the central superintendence which the Poor Law Board[18] is intended to exercise over the administrators of the Poor Rate throughout the country. Whatever powers the Board exercises beyond this limit were right and necessary in that peculiar case for the cure of rooted habits of maladministration in matters deeply affecting not the localities merely, but the whole community; since no locality has a moral right to make itself by mismanagement a nest of pauperism, necessarily overflowing into other localities and impairing the moral and physical condition of the whole laboring community. The powers of administrative coercion and subordinate legislation possessed by the Poor Law Board (but which, owing to the state of opinion on the subject, are very scantily exercised by them), though perfectly justifiable in a case of a first-rate national interest, would be wholly out of place in the superintendence of interests purely local. But a central organ of information and instruction for all the localities would be equally valuable in all depart-

---

* tribunals—tribunal (1859a, 1859b).

ments of administration. A government cannot have too much of the kind of activity which does not impede, but aids and stimulates, individual exertion and development. The mischief begins when, instead of calling forth the activity and powers of individuals and bodies, it substitutes its own activity for theirs; when, instead of informing, advising, and, upon occasion, denouncing, it makes them work in fetters or bids them stand aside and does their work instead of them. The worth of a state, in the long run, is the worth of the individuals composing it; and a state which postpones the interests of *their* mental expansion and elevation to a little more of administrative skill, or that semblance of it which practice gives, in the details of business; a state which dwarfs its men, in order that they may be more docile instruments in its hands even for beneficial purposes—will find that with small men no great thing can really be accomplished; and that the perfection of machinery to which it has sacrificed everything will in the end avail it nothing, for want of the vital power which, in order that the machine might work more smoothly, it has preferred to banish.

Notes to the Text

EPIGRAPH

1. Karl Wilhelm von Humboldt's (1767-1835) *The Sphere and Duties of Government* was written in 1792 but not published until 1851. An English translation of the work, by Joseph Coulthard, appeared in 1854; this epigraph is from p. 65 of that edition.

DEDICATION

1. Harriet Taylor Mill (1807-58), married to John Stuart Mill in 1851. See the editor's introduction pp. 16-8.

CHAPTER I:
INTRODUCTORY

1. Mill addressed the metaphysical dispute about the freedom of the human will—whether human choices and actions are free or causally determined in such a way as to preclude free will—in his *System of Logic*, Book 6, Chapter 2. See the editor's introduction, pp. 15-6.
2. Mill here alludes to the argument for absolute monarchy articulated by Thomas Hobbes (1599-1679) in *Leviathan* (1651).
3. The philosophical foundations of this approach to limiting political power were developed in John Locke's (1632-1704) *Second Treatise of Government* (1690).
4. This view is straightforwardly expressed in the American *Declaration of Independence* (1776) and the French *Declaration of the Rights of Man and Citizen* (1789).
5. In his *Social Contact* (1762), Jean-Jacques Rousseau (1712-78) argued that the collective citizenry of the state maintains inalienable sovereignty over itself and that the citizenry expresses itself through the general will, which has the public good as its sole object.
6. Among those liberal thinkers that Mill must certainly have had in mind here would be his own father, James Mill (1773-1836), and his father's close friend, Jeremy Bentham (1748-1832). See the editor's introduction pp. 5 ff. Mill would have also had in mind Continental thinkers such as Benjamin Constant (1767-1830), who played a leading role in the development of liberal ideology in France, and Wilhelm von Humboldt (1767-1835), whose liberal humanism deeply influenced Mill.
7. Mill is referring to the so-called Reign of Terror, the period of the French Revolution from September 1793-July 1794. During this period, the Revolutionary government,

under the direction of Maximilien de Robespierre (1758-1794), took extremely harsh measures against any suspected enemies of the Revolution, particularly members of the nobility and clergy. It is estimated that 300,000 individuals were arrested and 17,000 officially executed.

8. The United States of America.

9. *"the tyranny of the majority"*: The phrase is from Alexis de Tocqueville's *Democracy in America*, vol. I chpt. XV. See the editor's introduction, p. 12.

10. See, for example, James Madison's (1751-1836) *The Federalist No. 10: The Union as a Safeguard against Domestic Factions and Insurrection*. Madison and the framers of the United States Constitution were deeply concerned about the danger that majority rule poses in oppressing the freedom of the individual. Madison argued that a constitutional republic, better than a popular democracy, would protect the individual from the majority.

11. For example, de Tocqueville.

12. Mill is referring to moral intuitionism and proponents of that view such as Adam Sedgwick (1785-1873) and William Whewell (1794-1866). On moral intuitionism and Mill's arguments against this view, see the editor's introduction p. 14-5.

13. *Helots*: members of the serf class, essentially slaves, in the ancient Greek city-state of Sparta.

14. *roturiers*: people of low social rank: commoners.

15. *moral sense*: see the editor's introduction, p. 14 and 56 n.25.

16. *odium theologicum*: Latin, "religious hatred."

17. *Universal Church*: the Roman Catholic Church.

18. *dissentient*: one who disagrees with the opinion of the majority: a dissenter.

19. See, for example, John Locke's *A Letter on Toleration* (1689).

20. "Papist" is a (chiefly derogatory) term for a Roman Catholic. "Unitarian" refers to a member of any Christian sect that rejects the orthodox doctrine of the Trinity—the concept of three coequal persons, Father, Son, and Holy Ghost, in the Godhead—but believes in the oneness of God. While Unitarians deny the divinity of Jesus, they believe that he was a very important moral figure.

21. *remonstrating*: urging strong reasons against a course of action.

22. Mill's examples of enlightened despots. At the height of his power, the Mughal emperor Jalal un-Din Muhammad Akbar, or Akbar the Great, (1542-1605) controlled an empire spanning Northern India. Akbar abolished slavery, imposed a policy of religious toleration, and promoted commerce, literature, the arts and sciences. By the early-9th century C.E., Charlemagne, or Charles the Great, (742-814) controlled most of Christian Western Europe. He promoted commercial, intellectual, and cultural endeavors to such an extent that the period of his reign has come to be known as the Carolingian Renaissance.

23. On this passage, see the editor's introduction pp. 20 ff.

24. *primâ facie*: Latin, "at first sight" or "on its face." A prima facie case is one in which the initial evidence is sufficient to prove the case unless contradictory evidence is subsequently introduced.

25. *de jure*: Latin, "by law."

26. The Puritans were a group of English Protestants of the late-16th and 17th centuries who sought to purify—hence, the name—the Church from unscriptural doctrines, rituals, and practices. Over time, 'Puritanism' came to refer to the practice of strict religious or moral behavior generally.

27. The French philosopher and sociologist Auguste Comte (1798-1857) is known as the founder of positivism—a doctrine in terms of which he attempted to define the proper political arrangements for modern industrial society in his *Système de politique positive* (*System of Positive Polity*, 4 vols; 1851-4). According to Comte, human thought and society evolve through certain distinct stages, which he called the theological or religious, the metaphysical, and the positive or scientific. In the theological stage (characterized by

medieval Europe) phenomena are ultimately explained in terms of god(s); later, in the metaphysical stage (characterized by Europe during the Scientific Revolution), phenomena are explained in terms of unseen forces; finally, in the positive stage (which Comte thought Europe was just starting to enter during his lifetime), explanations are based solely on verifiable observations. Among the features of the positive society that Comte imagines is a "religion of humanity" in which historical figures are worshipped according to their contribution to society. Though Mill was sympathetic to Comte's fundamental contention that social problems should be studied and addressed scientifically, he accused Comte of "liberticide" in designing his positivist utopia. For Mill's assessment of Comte's thought, see his essay "Auguste Comte and Positivism" in *Collected Works* vol. 10.

CHAPTER II:
OF THE LIBERTY OF
THOUGHT AND DISCUSSION

1. The House of Tudor ruled England from 1485 (Henry VII) to 1603 (Elizabeth I).
2. A Churchman is a member of the Church of England; a Buddhist is an adherent to the religion founded by Siddhartha, who flourished in Northern India in the 5th century B.C.E.; and a Confucian is a follower of the teachings of the Chinese philosopher Confucius (551-479 B.C.E.). Peking is the traditional English name for Beijing—the capital of China.
3. *gainsayers*: those who deny or to speak against.
4. *"devil's advocate"*: The Devil's Advocate (Latin, *Advocatus Diaboli*) is the official whose function it is to put the case *against* beatification or canonization by the Roman Catholic Church.
5. *Newtonian philosophy*: the mechanical philosophy of Isaac Newton (1642-1727).
6. Thomas Carlyle "Memoirs of the Life of Scott" *London and Westminster Review* (Jan., 1838, p. 315).
7. The Greek philosopher Socrates (c.469-399 B.C.E.) challenged his fellow Athenians to submit their moral opinions to critical scrutiny. He was tried on charges of impiety and corrupting the youth. Found guilty, he was put to death. Socrates' personality and views were immortalized in the early dialogues of his student Plato (c.428-347 B.C.E.). Plato's influence on the Western philosophical tradition is rivaled only by that of his own greatest student, Aristotle (384-322 B.C.E.).
8. *"i maëstri di color che sanno"*: Italian for "the masters of those who know." An allusion to Dante's *Divine Comedy, Inferno* IV.131.
9. The events surrounding the trial and death of Socrates are presented in three of Plato's dialogues. The *Apology* presents an idealized account of Socrates' defense at his trial; the *Crito* presents Socrates' reasons for refusing to escape from prison after his conviction; and the *Phædo* recounts Socrates' final hours and death. Socrates' accuser, to whom Mill here refers, was Meletus.
10. *Calvary*: the site of the crucifixion of Jesus.
11. Caiaphas. See Matthew 26:57-66.
12. Born Saul of Tausus (died c.67 C.E.). See Acts 8:1.
13. Caesar Marcus Aurelius Antoninus Augustus (121-80) was one of the most respected emperors in Roman history. He discharged his public duties with great diligence and devoted himself to the study of law and philosophy, especially Stoicism—an ancient Greek school of philosophy founded by Zeno of Citium (c.336-c.265 B.C.E.) that is known for its austere ethical doctrines.
14. Constantine I, or Constantine the Great, (c.274-337) became emperor of the Western Roman Empire after his victory over Maxentius in 312. Believing that the victory was

the work of the Christian God, he became the first emperor to promote Christianity. His Edict of Milan (313)—offered jointly with Licinius, the emperor of the East—brought toleration to Christians throughout the Empire. Constantine became the sole emperor of the Empire after defeating Licinius in 324.

15. Samuel Johnson (1709-84), British lexicographer and critic. In his *Life of Johnson*, James Boswell records the following conversation between Johnson and a certain Reverend Dr. Mayo on the subject of toleration: "JOHNSON: 'Every society has a right to preserve public peace and order, and therefore has a good right to prohibit the propagation of opinions which have a dangerous tendency....Every man has a right to liberty of conscience, and with that the magistrate cannot interfere. People confound liberty of conscience with liberty of talking—no, with liberty of preaching. Every man has a physical right to think as he pleases, for it cannot be discovered how he thinks. He has not a moral right, for he ought to inform himself and think justly. But, Sir, no member of a society has a right to teach any doctrine contrary to what that society holds to be true. The magistrate, I say, may be wrong in what he thinks; but, while he thinks himself right, he may and ought to enforce what he thinks.' MAYO: 'Then, Sir, we are to remain always in error and truth can never prevail; and the magistrate was right in persecuting the first Christians.' JOHNSON: 'Sir, the only method by which religious truth can become established is by martyrdom. The magistrate has a right to enforce what he thinks; and he who is conscious of the truth has a right to suffer. I am afraid there is no other way of ascertaining the truth, but by persecution on the one hand and enduring it on the other.'" (May 7, 1773—modified, ed.).

16. Locri, a Greek colony in southern Italy, is reputed to have had the first written legal code in Europe. After the code was established, its author, Zaleucus (fl. 660 B.C.E.), instituted the practice that Mill describes here. See Demosthenes' "Against Timocrates" 24.139.

17. The German priest and theologian Martin Luther (1483-1546) is regarded as the initiator of the Protestant Reformation, but as Mill indicates here, numerous reform movements, which were sharply, and often violently, suppressed, preceded Luther's. Arnold of Brescia (c.1100-55), a critic of the Church's wealth and temporal power, was executed for his involvement in an insurrection against the papal government. Fra Dolcino of Navario (d.1307) was burned at the stake for his anticlerical views and activities. The Italian priest Girolamo Savonarola (1452-1498), who criticized Church corruption and briefly led the democratic Florentine Republic, was hanged for heresy. The Albigeois, or Albigensians—members of a heretical Christian sect that flourished in southern France in the late-12th century—were subjected to military crusades and persecution under the Inquisition. The Vaudois, or Waldensians, were followers of Peter Waldo (fl. 1175), a wealthy merchant who repudiated his lifestyle and sought to emulate the life of Jesus, preaching and living in poverty. The Vaudois initially attempted to operate within the strictures of the Church, but when they met with official criticism the Vaudois broke away, splitting with the Church on certain doctrinal issues. Waldo was excommunicated by Pope Lucius III, and the Vaudois were severely persecuted. The Lollards were followers of the British theologian John Wyclif (c.1330-84), who produced the first English translation of the Bible. Wyclif's critical views on the Church's wealth and power, and certain doctrines, such as transubstantiation, were condemned. The Bohemian theologian John Huss (c.1369-1415), a disciple of Wylcif, was excommunicated and burned at the stake. His execution sparked the Hussite Wars in the mid-15th century.

18. Queen Mary I (1516-1558) attempted to restore Catholicism in England after her father Henry VIII (1491-1547) broke with the Church. Upon her death, Mary's Protestant half-sister Elizabeth I (1533-1603) assumed the throne.

19. *sepulchers*: structures in a church for the storage of religious objects, sacraments, and relics.

20. *assizes*: periodic sessions held in each county of England and Wales for the administration of civil and criminal law.
21. *Old Bailey*: the seat of the Central Criminal Court in London.
22. *obloquy*: disgrace or humiliation.
23. *pecuniary*: financial.
24. *ad misericordiam*: Latin, "for mercy."
25. The first period Mill refers to here is the Renaissance—the great revival of art and letters, under the influence of classical models, which began in Italy in the 14th century and continued during the 15th and 16th. The second period is the Enlightenment, particularly as it is associated with the spirit and aims of the so-called *philosophes*—French philosophers such as Voltaire (1694-1788), Montesquieu (1689-1755), and Diderot (1713-84) who compiled the *Encyclopedia, or Classified Dictionary of Sciences, Arts, and Trades*, one of the major intellectual achievements of the century. The poet and dramatist Johann Wolfgang von Goethe (1749-1832) and the philosopher Johann Gottlieb Fichte (1762-1814) are representatives of the initial phase of the German Romantic Movement taking place in the late-18th and early-19th centuries.
26. "Natural philosophy" refers to what we now call natural science—the study of natural bodies and the phenomena connected with them. Ptolemy's (127-45) geocentric (earth-centered) theory of the universe held sway until dislodged by the heliocentric (sun-centered) theory of Nicolas Copernicus (1473-1543). According to the phlogiston theory of combustion expounded by the German physicist Georg Ernst Stahl (1660-1734), all combustible bodies contain phlogiston—a substance that is disengaged in the process of combustion. The theory was disproved by the French chemist Antoine Lavoisier (1743-94), who discovered oxygen. Belief in phlogiston was generally abandoned by 1800.
27. The Roman statesman Marcus Tullius Cicero (106-43 B.C.E.) was regarded as the greatest orator of the ancient world after the Greek Demosthenes (c.383-322 B.C.E.).
28. *nisi prius*: Latin, "unless before." An English legal term, used more generally to mean valid unless proven otherwise. A "*nisi prius* advocate," then, is one who takes the validity of his or her cause for granted.
29. *formularies*: statements drawn up in formulas.
30. These tenets can all be found in the Book of Matthew: 5:3; 19:24; 7:1; 5:34; 19:19; 5:40; 6:34; 19:21, respectively.
31. From the *Apology* of Tertullian (c.160-220).
32. The French Protestant theologian John Calvin (1509-64) founded and headed a theocracy in Geneva in the mid-16th century. The Scottish Protestant reformer John Knox (c.1513-72) founded the Presbyterian Church in 1560.
33. Unattributed quote in *Thoughts for the Cloister and Crowd* (London, 1835, p.21).
34. Scholasticism is a philosophical tradition that arose in the universities of medieval Europe and is associated with the methods and views of the major philosophers of the 13th and 14th centuries, including Aquinas, Scotus, and Ockham. Scholasticism dominated European philosophy into the 15th century. Students in this tradition were trained by engaging in disputations—exercises in which parties formally propose, attack, and defend a set question or thesis.
35. "*Socratici viri*": Latin, "Socratic men," *i.e.*, followers or disciples of Socrates.
36. *fronting*: confronting
37. Jean-Jacques Rousseau (1712-78) argued in works such as his *Discourse on the Arts and Sciences* (1750) and *Discourse on the Origin and Foundations of Inequality Amongst Men* (1755) that humans are naturally good, but are corrupted by the influences of civilization.
38. *enervating*: physically weakening.
39. *trammels*: things that impede, hinder, confine, or restrain.
40. See Paul's Letters to the Colossians (3:22-4:1) and the Ephesians (6:5-9) where he prescribes rules regulating the conduct of masters and slaves, but does not condemn the practice of slavery per se.

41. In fact this passage is not in the Koran (the sacred book of Islam).
42. *sophistically*: The Sophists of ancient Greece were paid teachers of rhetoric. Plato accused them of teaching their students to persuade others using clever but deceptive or fallacious arguments.
43. *calumny*: slander or defamation.
44. *vituperation*: abusive or harshly critical language.

CHAPTER III:
OF INDIVIDUALITY

1. On this passage, see the editor's introduction p. 36.
2. *savant*: French, "learned person."
3. *consentaneous to*: suitable or agreeable to.
4. *they like in crowds*: they approve of or take pleasure only in things that are liked by large groups of people.
5. *pollards*: trees whose tops have been cut off to encourage the growth of new branches.
6. On Knox, see Chapter II, n. 32. The Athenian statesman and general Alcibiades (c.450-404 B.C.E.) was a student of Socrates and a leader against Sparta in the Peloponnesian War. Notorious as a libertine, when he was recalled to Athens to stand trial for sacrilege he fled to Sparta and gave them advice that led to major Athenian defeats. Pericles (c.495-429 B.C.E.) helped to institute the constitutional reforms that brought about full Athenian democracy and presided over the Athenian "Golden Age."
7. *aliment*: sustenance.
8. The Byzantine, or Eastern Roman, Empire survived for a thousand years after the collapse of the Western Roman Empire. The Byzantine period spanned from 395-1453.
9. *ex vi termini*: Latin, "by the force of the term," *i.e.*, by definition.
10. The Niagara River is about 35 miles long and is the natural outlet from Lake Erie to Lake Ontario. The cascades at Niagara Falls vary from 70 to 170 feet.
11. The Scottish-born writer and historian Thomas Carlyle (1795-1881) defended such a position in his *Heroes, Hero-Worship, and the Heroic in History* (London, 1841).
12. commission *de lunatico*: a commission to determine soundness of mind.
13. Foot binding was a custom practiced in China for many centuries. Young girls' feet were tightly wrapped in bandages so that they would not grow normally. The bound feet remained small and dysfunctional.
14. Alexis de Tocqueville's (1805-59) *The Old Regime and the Revolution* (1856).
15. See pp. 112-3.

CHAPTER IV:
OF THE LIMITS TO THE
AUTHORITY OF SOCIETY OVER
THE INDIVIDUAL

1. Mill here rejects contractarianism—the theory that political relations and obligations originate in contract or voluntary agreement. This approach to political philosophy was developed by Thomas Hobbes (1588-1679) in *Leviathan* (1651), John Locke (1632-1704) in *Two Treatises of Government* (1690), and Jean Jacques Rousseau (1712-78) in *The Social Contract* (1762).
2. *obtruded*: forced or imposed (oneself or one's ideas) without request or permission.
3. "Pleonexia"—Greek, "greed" or "avarice."

4. Regarding the tenability of the distinction between "self-regarding" and "other-regarding" actions, see the editor's introduction pp. 46-7.
5. George Barnwell was the subject of a 17th century English ballad and George Lillo's morality play, *The London Merchant, or the History of George Barnwell* (1731).
6. In 1649 Oliver Cromwell (1599-1658) and the Puritans overthrew the monarchy, executed Charles I (1600-49), and established the English Commonwealth. Cromwell's reign was characterized by rigid discipline and strict morality. For example, theaters were closed and stage performances banned. The monarchy was restored in 1660 when Charles II (1630-85) ascended the throne. The reopening of theaters initiated a rebirth of English drama, and Restoration comedies are famous for their sexual explicitness. Charles II, "The Merry Monarch," exemplified the rakish, aristocratic ethos portrayed in these plays, and left at least 14 illegitimate offspring.
7. *Mohammedans*: Muslims. The term "Mohammedan" is regarded as offensive by many Muslims today to the extent that it suggests that a human being—the prophet Mohammed (570-632)—is the central focus of Islam, when, in fact, it is Allah.
8. *Calvinists and Methodists*: followers of the austere religious movements founded by John Calvin (see Chapter II, n. 32), and John Wesley (1703-91) and Charles Wesley (1707-88), respectively.
9. *sumptuary law*: a law regulating expenditures, particularly expenditures related to luxury goods.
10. *suppositious*: hypothetical or fictional.
11. Mill is referring to the Maine Liquor Law (1851), which was adopted by a number of States and presaged national prohibition in the United States.
12. The United Kingdom Alliance for the Legislative Suppression of the Sale of Intoxicating Liquors was founded in 1853. The correspondence that Mill refers to was between the Alliance's Secretary, Samuel Pope, and the British statesman Edward Henry Stanley (1826-93), Fifteenth Earl of Derby. See "Lord Stanley, M.P., and the United Kingdom Alliance," in *The Times*, Oct. 2· 1856, pp. 9-10.
13. *Sabbatarian legislation*: laws governing conduct on the Sabbath.
14. *emolument*: payment for work.
15. "*Deorum injuriæ Diis curæ*": Latin, "injuries to the gods can be cured by the gods." See Tacitus' *Annals* I.lxxiii.
16. *Mormonism*: A millenary Christian sect, the Church of Jesus Christ of Latter-Day Saints was founded by Joseph Smith (1805-44), who claimed to find and translate the *Book of Mormon* (1830), a text accepted by Mormons as Scripture along with the Bible. According to this text, Christ appeared and established his Church in the New World. Smith, as Mill indicates, was killed by a mob that broke into the jail where he was being held awaiting trial for conspiracy. The Mormons, led by Brigham Young (1801-77), fled to the American West to escape persecution, settling in Salt Lake City, Utah.
17. *imposture*: deception.
18. The Western Roman Empire was overrun by "Barbarians"—Vandals, Huns, Ostrogoths, Visigoths, and Suevi—in the 5th century C.E.

CHAPTER V:
APPLICATIONS

1. So, harm to others is a *necessary* but not a *sufficient* condition for political or social coercion.
2. The doctrine of free trade, or *laissez-faire*, received strong support in the classical school of economics that developed in Great Britain under the influence of Adam Smith (1723-90). Important works of this school include Smith's *An Inquiry into the Nature*

and Causes of the Wealth of Nations (1776), David Ricardo's (1772-1823) *Principles of Political Economy and Taxation* (1817), James Mill's *Elements of Political Economy* (1821), and John Stuart Mill's own *Principles of Political Economy* (1848).

3. *cæteris paribus*: Latin, "other things being equal."

4. p. 142 (See Chapter IV, n. 11).

5. The British East India Company exported opium grown in India to China in the 18th and 19th centuries. When addiction became a serious problem, China outlawed the importation and cultivation of opium. China's attempts to suppress the opium trade led to the Opium Wars of 1839-42 and 1856-60.

6. *punitory*: punitive.

7. See Bentham's *An Introductory View of the Rationale of Evidence* in *The Works of Jeremy Bentham*, Vol. VI, p. 60.

8. *public weal*: public welfare or wellbeing.

9. *à fortiori*: Latin, "with even stronger reason," *i.e.*, more conclusively.

10. *The Sphere and Duties of Government*. See pp. 112-3.

11. John Locke's (1632-1704) *Essay concerning Human Understanding* (1689) is regarded as a classic statement of British empiricism. The German philosopher Immanuel Kant (1724-1804) criticized empiricism, particularly as it was worked out by David Hume (1711-1776), and developed an alternative theory of knowledge in his *Critique of Pure Reason* (1781).

12. See n. 2 above.

13. See, for example, Mill's own essay "Reform of the Civil Service" (1854).

14. *Chinese mandarin*: an official in the civil service of the Chinese Empire.

15. *Jesuit*: a member of the Society of Jesus—a Roman Catholic order that was founded by Ignatius Loyola (c.1491-1556) in 1534 to defend the Church against the Reformation movement.

16. *mill-horse round*: the image here is of a horse endlessly walking the same circular path in order to turn the wheel of a mill.

17. *pedantocracy*: a government by pedants—persons excessively concerned with trifling details or strict adherence to formal rules. The term is apparently Comte's.

18. *Poor Law Board*: a body established to supervise the administration of the British Poor Law of 1834.

Index